fronts, offering a profound exploration of innovative practices that are key to achieving breakthrough results for modern charitable organizations."

**NATHAN CHAPPELL**

Co-author of *The Generosity Crisis: The Case for Radical Connection to Solve Humanity's Greatest Challenges*

"Essential reading for any nonprofit leader who wants to create a thriving organization. Innovation is hard. Gabe has pulled together some of the best frameworks and practices from both the nonprofit and for-profit worlds that can help illuminate a path forward in times of change."

**DAVE RALEY**

Founder, Imago Consulting

"Bursting with energy and expertise, this book is a goldmine of innovative practices, engaging stories, and practical tips to improve your fundraising efforts. Get ready to be inspired and invigorated! Whether you're a nonprofit pro or in the early stages of your career, you'll be equipped with the right strategies to transform your nonprofit's giving programs and build long-lasting relationships with your supporters."

**MAUREEN WALBEOFF**

Nonprofit Digital Strategist & Technology Expert
meetmaureen.com

"As someone who leads innovation for some of the largest nonprofits in the country, *The Responsive Nonprofit*, is the most practical guide to creating an organization of innovation. Buy a copy for everyone on your team now!"

**MARK MILLER**

Co-founder Historic Agency
Co-author of *Culture Built My Brand: The Secret to Winning More Customers Through Company Culture*

# THE
# RESP●NSIVE
# NONPROFIT

# THE RESPONSIVE NONPROFIT

## 8 Practices That Drive Nonprofit Innovation and Impact

virtuous

AUTHOR OF RESPONSIVE FUNDRAISING
### GABE COOPER

WITH SCOTT RICHARDS & BRYAN FUNK

liberalis

Published by Liberalis, an imprint of Brisance Books Group LLC

The publisher is not responsible for websites or their content that are not owned by the publisher.

Liberalis
Brisance Books Group
21001 N. Tatum Blvd
Suite 1630
Phoenix, AZ 85050

Printed in Canada

First Edition
April 2024
Hardcover

ISBN: 978-1-962988-14-8

052024

# CONTENTS

# ACKNOWLEDGMENTS

This book wouldn't have been possible without the collective wisdom of the amazing nonprofit leaders I've been blessed to work with over the past 20 years. Their dedication to the cause, and to the communities that they serve, provides me with a never-ending well of inspiration. Thank YOU for all of your amazing work.

A special thank you to the Virtuous team members (Bryan and Scott) and the nonprofit thought leaders who contributed their time and wisdom to help make this book possible. The ideas in this book are not new or novel. I'm happy to stand on the shoulders of the brilliant people who paved the path toward nonprofit innovation.

Thanks to Kellie for editing both of my books. Her patience and diligence made this book possible.

And finally, thanks to my family and friends. Everyone needs durable friendships to weather the ups and downs of life. Thanks to my wife Farrah for supporting me in my entrepreneurial journey. Thanks to the LX crew for inspiring me to swing big. And thanks to the world-class leaders at Virtuous for providing me with the bandwidth to write and dream.

# PART 1

# THE PROBLEM: KEEPING PACE IN A WORLD OF CONSTANT INNOVATION

# A VISION FOR RESPONSIVE NONPROFITS

*"Around here, however, we don't look backwards for very long. We keep moving forward, opening up new doors and doing new things, because we're curious…and curiosity keeps leading us down new paths." – Walt Disney*

Driving innovation at a nonprofit can often feel like a herculean task. Over the past 15 years, I've had front-row seats to observe thousands of nonprofit executives, fundraisers, and marketers navigate the challenges and triumphs associated with creating transformational change. I've had the privilege of watching forward-thinking nonprofit leaders beat the odds and create outsized impact for their cause. And, after a decade and a half of seeing innovative nonprofits in action, I'm still blown away by leaders who are able to dream big and produce new forms of impact in their communities.

But I've also seen firsthand how nonprofits can get overwhelmed by changes in the world around them, and eventually begin to die the slow death of irrelevance. As nonprofits grow, "institutional inertia" often sets in and the status quo is protected as sacred. Processes begin to calcify and risk-taking is discouraged. And, despite the increasing pace of change in the world around us, many nonprofits struggle to adapt quickly and maximize their impact.

If you know me, you know that I have a relentless desire to innovate and disrupt the status quo. For better or worse, I constantly ask "why" things work the way they do — and "how" we might improve them. As a result, a decade ago, I began to sense a growing curiosity around three critical questions related to nonprofit innovation:

1. How are the very best nonprofits continuing to drive increased generosity and innovation to tackle the world's toughest challenges?

2. Why are the top nonprofits succeeding where others fail?

3. What are the key inhibitors of innovation and change in the nonprofit space? And how can these inhibitors be overcome?

I've now asked a version of these questions to hundreds of top nonprofit leaders and consultants. As we've listened to nonprofit professionals, looked at the data, and watched the most innovative nonprofits in action, we've identified a set of eight operating practices that are shared by leading nonprofits. Most of these practices seem to be a consistent part of the operational DNA of the world's most impactful organizations.

There's no magic formula for success, and no nonprofit is perfect. That said, there is a clear correlation between the adoption of the practices in this book and the growth and health of a nonprofit.

If you're hoping for a "silver bullet" or a shiny novel idea, then this book isn't for you. The practices in this book are not new. Each of these eight practices represents a pressure-tested best practice for innovation. And while the practices themselves may seem relatively simple, they are not easy. Driving increased generosity, embracing innovation, and building healthy teams requires hard work. But it is possible! And my hope is that this book can provide a roadmap for innovation within your organization.

Each chapter in the book outlines one of the eight core practices for responsive nonprofit innovation, and then provides tactical advice on how to begin implementing change. I'm quick to acknowledge that I don't have all the answers, and my experience is incomplete. With that in mind, we've worked hard to interview some of the best innovators and leaders in the nonprofit sector. Each chapter includes interviews, stories, and insights that we've assembled from top nonprofit thought leaders, fundraising consultants, and nonprofit executives. I'm incredibly grateful for the collective wisdom shared by our collaborators and co-conspirators. Their hard-earned experience gives nuance and perspective to each practice, and helps create a clear view of what success looks like.

## THE PROBLEM: AN ACCELERATING PACE OF CHANGE

For decades, technology gurus, sociologists, and futurists have been describing both the problems and opportunities created by the acceleration of innovation in our world. In order to better understand the impact of this increased pace of change, many innovators consistently reference three immutable laws of innovation. Combined, these three laws paint a clear picture of the challenges nonprofits will face if they aren't willing to prioritize innovation as a core part of their culture.

### Immutable Law 1: Moore's Law

Early in my career as a software developer, I was introduced to Moore's Law (named for Intel Founder Gordon Moore). Moore's Law established that the speed of computer processing was doubling every two years, and it would continue doubling every two years for the foreseeable future.

At the time, many of Moore's contemporaries doubted that computer processing power would continue to accelerate at breakneck speeds. Most people simply didn't have the imagination to envision a world with seemingly infinite computer processing power. And they certainly didn't have a clear vision for what the rise of computing power would mean for the world. But now, 40 years later, the smartphone in your pocket is 5,000 times more powerful than the world's largest supercomputer in the '80s (the CRAY-2). Ultimately, Gordon Moore was right and, as a result, the world we live in will never be the same.

### Immutable Law 2: The Law of Accelerating Returns

In the early 2000s, Ray Kurzweil expanded Moore's Law by establishing "The Law of Accelerating Returns," which effectively said that ALL innovation is advancing exponentially over time. For Kurzweil, it wasn't just computer processing that was accelerating — it was every advancement in science, systems, and technology. He believed that advances in innovation are evolutionary and that each new advancement quickly builds on the shoulders of what came before it. I doubt that Kurzweil himself fully understood how prophetic his seminal work would become. Within a decade of his writing, the world saw the launch of the iPhone, social media,

Uber, and countless other game-changing innovations – each new technology quickly building on what came before.

### Immutable Law 3: Martec's Law

Finally, in 2014, technology expert Scott Brinker coined the term "Martec's Law" to describe the immutable reality that technology is accelerating faster than most organizations can adapt. This concept is likely the most underappreciated truth in the nonprofit sector. The law explains that, over time, innovation accelerates exponentially, while most businesses naturally slow down and resist change as they scale.

In Brinker's model, successful organizations acknowledge the innovation constraints associated with their scale and focus only on the innovation and technology that will have the most significant impact. Though this law was formally articulated in 2014, some version of this concept has been the driving force behind innovation for decades. The accelerating pace of innovation will perpetually create threats to more established organizations while providing new opportunities for up-and-coming disrupters.

Collectively, these three laws accurately describe a world that will continue to advance at a pace far beyond our collective imagination. They also help us understand how disruptive organizations like Apple, Google, Amazon, and others leverage accelerated innovation to create outsized impact and scale.

Unfortunately, we've also seen countless organizations succumb to the pressures created by these immutable laws of innovation. For every tech startup or nonprofit disrupting a market by driving game-changing innovation, there's another organization being crushed by the accelerating pace of change. A few examples of well-known, innovation-induced implosions in the for-profit sector include:

- KODAK infamously going down in flames in the late '90s because of their unwillingness to embrace digital photography.

- Toys-R-Us slowly sinking into bankruptcy after failing to capitalize on the growing world of e-commerce.

- Blockbuster video passing on the opportunity to buy Netflix and subsequently closing its doors because it completely underestimated the future potential of streaming video.

At the end of day, innovation will continue to accelerate — and only the most nimble organizations will survive. As much as organizations want to believe they are immune to disruption, we are all subject to an accelerating world that constantly threatens to make our work irrelevant.

Martec's Law, in particular, has increasing relevance in the world of nonprofits. Change often happens faster than our organizations can adapt. Charities are facing exponential changes in how donors interact with their cause, and in how they deliver their programs and services to the community. At the same time, nonprofit teams often lack the insights, capital, and culture of innovation required to keep pace with the changing world. As a result, more and more nonprofits are drifting into irrelevance as the world passes them by.

At its heart, this book is designed to be the antidote to Martec's Law for your nonprofit. The world needs the work that you do! And you can't afford to let the pace of innovation outside of your organization minimize your impact. The good news is that it's possible to beat the odds by building a culture of innovation within your nonprofit. With the right culture and practices in place, you have the ability to overcome the threats posed by a changing world and ride the wave of innovation toward increased impact.

## THE PREQUEL: THE RISE OF RESPONSIVE FUNDRAISING

Three years ago, I set out to write a fundraising-specific book to help answer a more limited version of the three core questions: How are leading fundraising teams driving increased generosity to tackle the world's toughest challenges? And why are the top nonprofit fundraisers/marketers succeeding?

In the years before writing *Responsive Fundraising*, we noticed that nonprofits were fundraising in a world that had fundamentally changed. The rise of social media, smartphones, and hyper-connected personalized brand experiences had forever changed how donors interact with the world around them.

Because of these macro-shifts, it was becoming harder to earn the attention of "everyday" donors, while more and more people were opting out of charitable giving altogether. A key driver of these trends seemed to be a growing distrust of institutions and inauthentic traditional marketing practices. Donors now EXPECTED a more personalized and authentic connection to the causes that they cared about most. They weren't less generous per se, they simply wanted to feel a real, personal connection to the cause.

In their book, *The Generosity Crisis*, Nathan Chappell and Brian Crimmins present a sobering case for the decline of generosity in

America. They argue that donors are less connected to nonprofit causes than ever before and that this disconnect may have far-reaching ramifications for both charities and culture at large if we are unwilling to change.

Harvard Professor and *New York Times* bestseller, Arthur C. Brooks, summed up their case well by saying, "The Generosity Crisis confronts us with alarming trends in charitable giving. But it isn't a bad news book about America. On the contrary, it shows us how donors and nonprofits can connect in new and better ways to inflect giving levels and lift each other up."

As we monitored the growing generosity crisis, we also noticed that a new breed of growth-oriented nonprofit fundraisers and marketers was beginning to emerge. These innovative leaders were using new tactics and technology to connect more personally with donors at scale. They were finding ways to listen to their donors and draw them into the frontlines of their work in more personal ways.

This new brand of "responsive" fundraising was breaking through the noise and driving outsized growth in generosity. Fundamentally, it acknowledged that prospective donors weren't any less generous than they used to be. But it also accepted that nonprofits needed to adopt new practices to better Listen to Donors, Connect Personally, and Suggest the Right Next Step for each person.

Over the past three years, I've received countless comments from fundraisers to say "thank you" for writing our first book. The resonance of *Responsive Fundraising* wasn't the result of our team introducing a "new idea." We simply provided a name and guidebook for what top fundraisers and marketers already implicitly knew to be true.

## THE RESPONSIVE NONPROFIT

As we've watched more nonprofits push toward a more responsive and connected approach to fundraising, we've found that many of the roadblocks to increased generosity aren't related to fundraising tactics or strategy at all. Most inhibitors to growing generosity were actually related to larger operational and cultural issues within nonprofit teams. Fundraisers and marketers WANT to be more responsive to donors, but the "operating system" of their organization dramatically hinders their ability to innovate and change.

To be successful in this new world, nonprofits must be able to effectively answer my third key question for themselves: *"What are the key inhibitors of innovation and change in the nonprofit space? And how can these inhibitors be overcome?"* And, as I said, the roadblocks to success run far deeper than fundraising or marketing tactics. To truly accelerate, nonprofits must relentlessly drive innovation and team effectiveness across the organization. They must align their team around a common mission, create a data-driven culture, and be willing to take measured risks to increase their impact.

Rather than narrowly focusing on fundraising and marketing, we've attempted to take a broader view in this book to address the organizational barriers to innovation. While the practices in this book can undoubtedly accelerate Fundraising teams, they will be most effective when applied across the entire organization.

This book is designed for nonprofit leaders who are ready to disrupt the status quo. It's time to break down the walls that stand in the way of sacrificial generosity and increased impact!

# THE KEY PRACTICES OF A RESPONSIVE NONPROFIT

*"Intelligence is traditionally viewed as the ability to think and learn. Yet in a turbulent world, there's another set of cognitive skills that might matter more: the ability to rethink and unlearn." – Adam M. Grant*

Over the past ten years, I've come to believe that eight core practices mark the most responsive and innovative nonprofits. Some organizations have adopted different flavors of these practices or have applied other names to their processes than I've outlined in this book. And, in some cases, many innovative nonprofits don't even have the language to describe "why they do what they do." Instead, through experimentation and pragmatism, they've evolved into efficient, innovative machines without a clear playbook or defined process.

If this is you, congrats! You're among the select few nonprofits who have cracked the code on innovation through sheer force of will. But, I suspect that most of my readers aren't in this category.

This book is for the rest of us. It's for the nonprofit that still has work to do in their innovation journey. It's for the nonprofit that sees sparks of innovation within its team but is unable to scale meaningful change. It's for the nonprofit leader who needs the language, practices, and playbook to more quickly usher in the new reality that they can see just over the horizon.

The responsive practices outlined below are all interrelated, but each chapter in this book has been written to stand alone. Feel free to jump forward to the practices that you feel might be most helpful — but make sure to circle back to the practices that you skip.

The first five innovation practices are focused on organizational effectiveness. They present tactical suggestions for team management, technology, goal setting, and developing your "innovation muscle."

The next two practices focus on creating a culture of innovation along with a loyal, story-driven community to help accelerate growth. While these practices might feel more "touchy feely," culture and community are the backbone of durable growth.

Finally, the eighth practice introduces a new team within your organization that can quarterback innovation and create a more holistic view of generosity.

I've provided a summary of each core practice below. It's time to jump in and begin building toward a more innovative and responsive future!

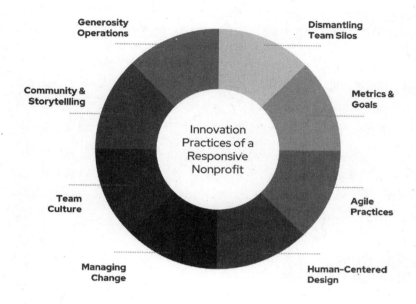

## PRACTICE 1:
## REMOVING SILOS AND INCREASING TRANSPARENCY

As we've worked with nonprofit teams, we've commonly discovered significant walls between departments and data sources within the organization. A lack of collaboration between teams, along with a dedication to the "way we have always done it," contribute to these walls. As a result, each individual team (and their data) becomes sealed off from other teams until they've functionally created their own mini kingdoms. For a nonprofit to become responsive, they must first dismantle these team and data silos and focus on creating a culture of transparency, adaptability, and collaboration. This practice provides the tactics and rationale for breaking down silos in order to drive more effective teams, accelerated innovation, and increased impact.

## PRACTICE 2:
## METRICS AND QUARTERLY GOAL SETTING

At for-profit organizations like Virtuous, we say that every team member should "know their number." In other words, everyone on the team should understand the specific metric they are responsible for. Unfortunately, many nonprofits are inhibited by unclear goals or invisible metrics. To be effective, nonprofits must align on the overarching goals and mission that everyone in the organization shares. This practice lays the foundation for goal setting and tracking KPIs to drive clear results.

## PRACTICE 3:
## THE AGILE NONPROFIT

If the past decade has taught us anything, it's that effective nonprofits must become more agile. In fact, the word "pivot" has become a standard part of the nomenclature at the most successful nonprofits that I work with. The Agile Methodology provides a time-tested framework for how nonprofits can systemize "agility" within their organization. This practice provides suggestions for how to organize your teams, meetings, and culture to quickly respond to changes in a way that honors both your donors and the communities that you serve.

## PRACTICE 4:
## HUMAN-CENTERED DESIGN

Driving meaningful impact requires working together in lockstep with your donors, volunteers, and communities that you serve. Human-Centered Design is a framework and mindset that puts your actual stakeholders at the center of your program and fundraising efforts. It helps establish a continuous feedback loop with your community — and creates strong organizational empathy with the people you serve. This practice introduces the foundation of great design thinking and how you can use authentic feedback from your stakeholders to jumpstart innovation.

## PRACTICE 5:
## MANAGING CHANGE

The only constant in today's world is change. Developing fluidity and adaptability with your organization could be the most important component of your success. Adopting new technology, dealing with team turnover, or shifting your program work all have the potential to dramatically slow your organization unless you have a clear strategy for change management. In this practice, we'll examine the importance of aligned goals and incentives, and look at examples of simple tactics that can help de-risk change.

## PRACTICE 6:
## BUILDING A DURABLE TEAM CULTURE

A healthy organizational culture is the gasoline that fuels team effectiveness. As nonprofits, we are sometimes so focused on the cause that we neglect the health and growth of our teams. This practice provides helpful frameworks and tactics for defining, communicating, and celebrating your organization's unique culture. It also touches on hiring and firing based on culture, and reinforcing culture at every level of the organization.

## PRACTICE 7:
## THE POWER OF COMMUNITY AND STORYTELLING TO DRIVE CHANGE

Nonprofits often feel under-resourced and under-staffed. At the same time, they often fail to recognize the massive untapped potential of their community. Your donors, volunteers, and advocates represent an army of raging fans ready to change the world. Creating a movement that unlocks the time, talent, and skills of your community can be the key to unlocking exponential growth. But building a movement requires great storytelling. Stories are the way that you communicate the vision for your cause — and tap into deeper meaning within your constituents. This practice examines how nonprofits can drive innovation and growth through storytelling and community building. And it examines the Invisible Children's KONY2012 campaign, Patagonia, Water.org, and other examples of how innovation has intersected with a story-driven community to drive outsized impact.

## PRACTICE 8:
## GENEROSITY OPERATIONS — STRUCTURING YOUR TEAM FOR SHARED INSIGHTS

One of the most common roadblocks for generosity is the need for shared insights throughout the organization. Siloed organizations are often encumbered by disparate and disconnected data and technology. In this practice, we'll discuss the value of a new kind of nonprofit team called Generosity Operations. This team sits outside of the other departments and focuses on creating centralized reporting, data sharing, and visible metrics across all teams. The result is increased team-wide alignment around common KPIs, and clear, data-driven decision-making.

# PART 2

# ESSENTIAL PRACTICES OF A RESPONSIVE NONPROFIT

# DISMANTLING TEAM SILOS AND INCREASING TRANSPARENCY

*"To tear down silos, leaders must go beyond behaviors and address the contextual issues at the heart of departmental separation and politics. Silos — and the turf wars they enable — devastate organizations. They waste resources, kill productivity, and jeopardize the achievement of goals. But beyond all that, they exact a considerable human toll too. They cause frustration, stress, and disillusionment by forcing employees to fight bloody, unwinnable battles with people who should be their teammates. There is perhaps no greater cause of professional anxiety and exasperation — not to mention turnover — than employees having to fight with people in their own organization. Understandably and inevitably, this bleeds over into their personal lives, affecting family and friends in profound ways." – Patrick Lencioni*

Early in our marriage, my wife worked as a program manager at a large homeless shelter. The organization (who shall remain nameless) had a great reputation in the community, and they continue to do great work to this day. Despite their amazing outward appearances,

I soon found out that there were serious systemic problems lurking just beneath the surface.

A few months into her job, my wife began to come home from work and tell me sobering stories of staff burnout and cynicism. The tenure of program managers, in particular, was incredibly short. And those who stuck around on the Program team for more than a couple of years typically became so jaded that they were ineffective in their job.

One day, after she vented her frustration, I asked my wife, "What does the leadership team think about these problems? Are they aware of the issues? Are people from other departments doing their part to make things better?"

Her answer to my question shocked me. She said "I don't know, we never really see anyone else from the organization. The other teams and leadership sit in a building on the other side of the parking lot, and we don't ever go over there. And they certainly don't come over to where we work."

Even in my early twenties with very little real work experience, her response seemed utterly unacceptable. Caring for people is hard enough as it is. In order to endure as a program manager at a homeless shelter, it seemed essential to have the support of both leadership and a broader team. The idea that a parking lot was creating a physical barrier between the Program team and the rest of the organization was mind-blowing.

The younger, naive me assumed that my wife's situation must be unique. It couldn't possibly be that other nonprofit organizations operated in similar silos with such substantial cultural disconnects.

Unfortunately, as I began working with more organizations, I realized that my wife's situation wasn't the exception…it was the rule. Only the most forward-thinking organizations worked cross functionally, collaborating and creating consistent team-wide community and culture.

The fact is that team silos represent one of the biggest hurdles to effectiveness at many nonprofits. As nonprofits grow and age, invisible walls begin to form within the organization that inhibit clear communication and slow down execution. Individual teams focus all of their energy on their specific problems and goals — and quickly lose sight of the broader organizational objectives. Individual contributors stop communicating with their peers on other teams. And, in the worst cases, resentment builds as mini kingdoms begin to form within the organization.

These organizational walls are often hardened by a lack of data transparency across the organization. The Fundraising, Program, IT, and Marketing departments work with software and spreadsheets that rarely talk with each other. Data is locked in silos and each team becomes less aware of how their work impacts the work on other teams.

These silos often go unnoticed. Like a frog slowly boiling in a pot of water, team members fail to notice as they slowly drift away from the broader organization and into their own walled-off world. Rarely do they take the time to step outside of their daily tasks to ask a peer on another team, "What are you working on? How can I help?"

Until these silos are removed and the organization unites as a single, cohesive organism moving in the same direction, growth will be stymied. In fact, most of the remaining practices laid out in this book will fail to succeed — at least not to the level they could — if your nonprofit teams remained siloed. Your organization will sputter and stall as frustrations and resentments build.

## DEPARTMENTAL GAPS

At Virtuous, we work with thousands of nonprofit professionals, and from our vantage point we have seen consistent patterns emerge around how walls form between nonprofit departments. For the sake of simplification, there are typically five distinct roles or departments in most nonprofits:

- Fundraising (Major Gifts, Direct Response, Events, etc)
- Program
- Communications/Marketing (sometimes rolled into Fundraising)
- Operations (Finance, Operations, IT, HR, etc)
- Volunteer

These five departments represent core building blocks for a nonprofit's growth engine. When these departments work in unison with shared goals and strong collaboration, it's like watching a highly tuned F1 race car with every piston firing at the same time to generate maximum horsepower.

But, more often than I'd like to admit, the departments are more like the engine of a 1975 Ford Pinto that is in desperate need of a tune-up. Pistons are firing at the wrong time or not all. The organization is constantly stalled. Parts are endlessly being replaced.

And organizational velocity never reaches 50 miles an hour as the rest of the world speeds by.

I'm probably pushing the car analogy a little too far at this point, but I have a story that helps illustrate how nonprofits typically deal with these challenges. When my wife and I were first dating, we didn't have two nickels to rub together. And we certainly didn't have enough money to drive a nice car. At the time, I drove an orange 1986 four-cylinder Ford Mustang. It looked like a Mustang on the outside, but the motor was only slightly bigger than our lawn mower engine. One of the idiosyncrasies of my Mustang is that it would constantly stall. In order to get it restarted, Farrah (my now wife) would have to get out of the car and push it down the street while I cranked the ignition and shifted into first gear. The car would lurch forward and Farrah would run alongside the car Mission Impossible-style and jump in.

So what does that story have to do with nonprofits? Glad you asked! As nonprofit teams begin to silo and become less effective, there are typically a few courageous (or crazy) team members who put on a cape, get out of the car, and push. These team members are usually lauded as heroes for going above and beyond. They put in long hours to pick up the slack of other teams in order to deliver results.

While it feels good to be the hero for a season, no one can wear a cape forever. Eventually, burnout will set in and resentment will grow. Fortunately, my wife put up with my nonsense and pushed my car — and still stuck around to marry me. But she's certainly the exception. When you look around your organization and see a few team members wearing capes to fill in the gaps caused by team disconnects, you can almost guarantee that breakdown and burnout are on the horizon.

## WHAT SILOS LOOK LIKE IN PRACTICE

I'm sure that you're already beginning to think of examples of silos within your team. In order to further spur your imagination, I'll provide a few specific examples of where we've seen team breakdowns begin to develop.

*We've seen Donor Development teams separated from the Program and Volunteer teams. In many cases, the Donor Development has very little visibility into the real "on the ground" impact of the organization. The result is inauthentic fundraising conversations and a disconnected donor experience that pushes donors further away from the cause.*

*We've seen Marketing and Communications departments who don't spend regular time with the Program team. As a result, the stories that get used in the marketing campaigns begin to feel cold or reused. Rather than marketing messages communicating an emotional, first-person experience, the messaging feels generic and vague.*

*We've seen the Fundraising team raise money for program-related projects without first collaborating with the Program team to ensure they can produce the necessary outcome data, making it difficult to close the loop with donors on their specific impact.*

*We've seen the Volunteer team disconnected from broader fundraising goals and donor information, resulting in unrealized donation dollars from volunteers... and unrealized volunteer hours from donors.*

*We've seen the Finance or Executive Team cut critical items from the budget because they lack visibility into how dollars are being used to increase impact or generosity across the organization.*

*We've seen organizations paying for three different email marketing tools and four different project management tools because IT is backlogged and teams aren't talking to each other. Purchase decisions are made in a vacuum because collaboration isn't worth the hassle.*

Any of this sound familiar?

Many nonprofits live in a state of disconnection. They default to Excel spreadsheets for managing their key data. They have very few cross-departmental meetings or shared goals. And only a select few staff truly understand how all the departments fit together, resulting in frustration and lack of empathy between the teams.

If any of these disconnects are true of your organization, it can feel like an internal tug-of-war for access, resources, and data. And the longer this struggle drags on, the more hardened your silos will become.

Unfortunately, these silos don't just impact your internal teams. They also affect your donors, volunteers, and the communities that you serve. The lack of organizational collaboration isolates donors and volunteers from the cause. The walls within your organization extend to become walls between your team and constituents.

Think about the last time you visited your favorite vacation spot. The desk associate who checked you in likely wasn't working the last time you visited, but she still knows to say "Welcome back Tina" rather than simply "Welcome" because they can see your guest record in their system. The hotel knows that celebrating your return is vital to your experience, so they make it easy for each associate to learn as much about you as possible. They diligently use shared data across their booking and check-in teams to drive exceptional client experiences.

Engaging with your favorite nonprofit should feel even MORE personal than your favorite hotel. But providing a personalized experience requires relentless collaboration across your teams — and a focus on the details. In nonprofit work, the details matter.

The people who engage with your cause aren't just one-dimensional rows in a database. I've worked with nonprofits where constituents have benefitted from the program work AND donated AND volunteered AND taken part in advocacy campaigns. Each person who engages with your nonprofit has their own story. And their involvement with your cause is both personal and varied. Your constituents EXPECT that each of your departments will understand their history and involvement with your organization. They don't see your departments as separate, freestanding units. And they expect a single coherent experience with your cause.

But when your teams are siloed and data isn't shared, your constituents can feel like they're interacting with completely different organizations. Essential insights are lost, messaging is fragmented, and your community feels disconnected.

## GETTING SPECIFIC: THE IT AND FUNDRAISING SILOS

While these problems can exist within any nonprofit team, they are often most acutely experienced within the IT and Fundraising departments. These two teams, in particular, exhibit distinct cultures that often isolate them from other teams. Both of these teams often hire team staff with very specific skills and mindsets that can seem disconnected from the actual work of the cause. I've worked with countless organizations who have described both the IT and Fundraising teams as "necessary evils" within the organization. While IT teams are viewed as a "speed bump" to getting anything done, Fundraisers are viewed as glorified "salespeople" who do the dirty work of bringing in money.

To be clear, I do IT for a living (I am a software developer by trade), and I actively fundraise for several nonprofits. I've somehow managed to land in both "necessary evil" camps. And, while I resent both of the stereotypes, I completely understand why they exist. If an organization lacks collaboration, shared goals, and empathy, then they will inevitably default to the most harmful stereotypes for roles that they don't fully understand.

## THE IT SILO

I can't tell you the number of times I've heard statements like, "I can't see our donor data because our IT team doesn't allow it" or, "I can't join your Slack group because our IT doesn't allow it" or, "Our IT team chose our Donor/Marketing/Accounting Software for us." In the name of "locking down security" or "creating consistency," countless IT teams have forced bad solutions on nonprofits, becoming a bureaucratic wet blanket on growth by creating neverending data projects.

To be clear, this isn't true of all nonprofit IT teams. There are plenty of fantastic, forward-thinking IT leaders in the nonprofit sector who relentlessly remove roadblocks for other teams. But in many nonprofits, IT teams have become synonymous with overreaching control and a painfully slow pace.

The other key practices in this book provide practical steps that can help align IT teams to the broader goals of the organization. But for now, we thought it might be helpful to provide a few paradigm shifts that may help break down the traditional IT silo. These simple adjustments can go a long way towards integrating the IT team back into the larger organization.

1. **IT doesn't own software purchase decisions** – In the for-profit world, the idea that software choices should lie solely with IT largely died in the late 1990s. For-profit companies realized that in order to be effective, teams needed the power to choose their own technology stack (in alignment with adjacent teams). In the nonprofit world, however, many IT teams still call the shots when it comes to technology choices. The most successful nonprofits allow the Program, Marketing, and Fundraising teams to choose their own technology. IT's role is to a) support the buying process with insights and helpful questions and, b) help explore how this decision might impact other departments (to avoid creating an unnecessary data silo).

2. **Any IT Initiative should be tied directly to a measurable organizational goal and have clear ROI in less than one year** – By having IT stack rank their projects based on organizational outcomes and ROI, you can often

avoid broad-reaching projects that deliver little value for the teams.

3. **Hire hackers, not craftsmen** – Nonprofits often default to hiring more seasoned IT leaders who spent most of their careers in larger corporate structures. These "experienced" leaders love the craft of IT, but they often aren't accustomed to getting stuff done in the modern world of technology. While the wisdom provided by these leaders can be helpful, they often lack the creativity and hands-on experience with newer technologies to be successful. Your IT team should include at least one scrappy "hacker" who is able to leverage modern tools to get work done quickly. In the words of software guru Jason Lempkin, you need a couple of "pirates and romantics" on your IT team!

## THE FUNDRAISING SILO

Generosity is at the heart of every nonprofit. Unfortunately, many nonprofits don't see their Fundraising team as a core part of their mission. Fundraising is often seen as the unsavory work that's needed in order to do the "real work" of the cause. Asking for money is often viewed as an uncomfortable (and sometimes sleazy) necessity. As a result, Fundraising teams are sometimes excluded from more "mission-focused" activities and separated from other teams.

In fact, we've seen organizations where the Fundraising team sits in a completely different office so that they don't disrupt the work of the organization.

This type of thinking completely misses the true heart of generosity and its power to accomplish great things for the cause. Generosity is at the very core of your mission. It's not a means to an end; it's part of the end itself. With that in mind, there are two practices and paradigm shifts needed to prevent this wall from forming within your organization:

1. **Generosity creates profound impact in the world AND profound impact in the heart of the giver** – Donating to your nonprofit has a double bottom-line impact. It not only funds your cause, but it transforms the heart of your donor. When your donors give, they become less focused on themselves and more focused on their neighbor. And, in many cases, they become your cause's most vocal advocates in their community. Rather than being a necessary evil, your Fundraising team is a catalyst that pushes your cause forward in your community and the culture at large. Your impact and your donors' giving are symbiotic parts of the same whole. This idea needs to be communicated clearly across your entire organization and baked into your culture. Your team needs to be consistently reminded that your Fundraising team and donors not only fund your programs, but are the hands and feet of your cause within the community. They are vital to pushing the mission forward.

2. **There's no rule against having Fundraisers help with Program, and Program staff help with Fundraising** – The most successful organizations that we've worked with have been diligent about blurring the line between Program and Fundraising. Program staff are tasked with calling to thank

donors every month (I talk more about this in my first book *Responsive Fundraising*). Meanwhile, Fundraisers allocate time every month to serve shoulder-to-shoulder with the Program team. This type of collaboration not only opens the lines of communication between your teams, but it also creates empathy for the Fundraising team and builds donor-facing generosity into the DNA of your entire organization. Whenever possible, try to include Program and Marketing staff in Fundraising planning meetings. Create space for input from the various teams. In the same way, allow the Fundraising team early access to new Program initiatives, and invite them to participate in Program team meetings.

I recently chatted with a nonprofit professional who served at World Vision, a prominent child sponsorship organization, during some of their most impressive growth years. He mentioned that World Vision never went onsite to evaluate a new program opportunity without bringing along someone from the Fundraising or Marketing team. Their approach was: "We need to determine how to do the work, how to fund the work, and how to tell the story all from the very beginning."

I absolutely love World Vision's approach. It perfectly illustrates the strategic nature of nonprofit fundraising and the importance of collaboration. Program, Fundraising, and Communications are symbiotic pieces of the same whole. And the more teams can strategically align their efforts from the beginning, the more influential the work will ultimately be.

## PRIORITIZING COLLABORATION: A CONVERSATION WITH THE EXPERTS

Heather Hiscox helps social impact organizations break down silos, improve team culture, and drive innovation through her organization Pause for Change. Heather's book *No More Status Quo: A Proven Framework to Change the Way We Change the World* is one of the most helpful resources I've found for creating a culture of empathy, collaboration, and innovation within a nonprofit.

We sat down with Heather to talk about the importance of creating connections and collaboration within nonprofit teams, and she shared some incredible insights.

"It's ironic, but I think one of the reasons we don't really create deep change in our organizations is that we work in disconnection," she says. "We don't have the time or space to think critically and have self-awareness. We often don't even know what people in our own office are doing."

In Heather's experience, when a nonprofit has internal disconnection, they aren't able to adequately serve their donors, volunteers, or the communities they support. That disconnection ripples out and has a huge impact on the work they do and the cause they're championing.

"It hurts their internal culture and it hurts the way they provide services in the community. As well as their ultimate success, potential funding, relationships with donors, success with grants, and all those things."

When Heather encounters a team struggling with organizational chaos as part of her consulting practice, she asks each person to consider two questions:

1. How do you make work harder or easier for another individual?

2. How do they make your life harder or easier?

These questions force each person on the team to consider how their individual contribution impacts the broader team. They begin to understand how their work ripples out and makes an impact on other teams' ability to operate at a higher level. Often, they find that the source of many of their biggest frustrations and obstacles is their inability to communicate empathetically with other people in their own organization.

I've personally been involved at nonprofits where poor team communication creates mountains of unnecessary work. For example, I've seen data entry teams spend hours of extra time manually entering data because the direct response team didn't include the proper data ID field on a printed response device. When I asked, "Why don't you just look up the account using an ID rather than type in all the data?" the answer was: "I don't know, the direct response team just doesn't print that field for us." Rather than asking "why" or collaborating with the other teams, many nonprofits are content to live with the inefficiencies built into the status quo.

"People just have to understand how they are all interconnected in the work," Heather Hiscox explains. "It's not an 'us' and 'them' — it's, 'let's get the family together and figure out how to get this done.'"

"But," she adds, "you have to provide the opportunities for people to connect, to understand what each person does. It has to be woven into the culture of the organization where there's time and space for that."

Maureen Wallbeoff, a well-respected nonprofit technologist and change agent, reinforces Hiscox's ideas when consulting nonprofits on technology adoption. Wallbeoff is quick to point out that, in the world of software change, empathy and cross-team collaboration are paramount. "If you are resisting feedback from other system users, things are going to fall apart. It won't be adopted across the organization. You're going to create workarounds immediately, which is never a great way to start using a new system."

"One of the practices that can work really well is just starting with some cross-functional governance," Wallbeoff explains. "You bring in a representative from all the different teams and departments, even Finance. Once a month, you spend an hour talking about technology, talking about results, talking about data, and collaboratively deciding what you're going to do. This way, things are happening *with you*, not to you. Because it can feel like that. Marketing is told what's going to happen, and the Program team is told how this is going to go, and it makes them very resistant. We all respond much better, and our end results are always better, when we work together than when we're flying solo in a vacuum."

## LET'S GET PRACTICAL

The remaining practices will provide you with more tactical recommendations for increasing departmental collaboration. But to get you started, we'd recommend experimenting with the following simple tactics to begin tearing down team walls.

Try out each of these small changes to see what works best for your team. There's sure to be some pushback on these changes initially, but hang in there! Change is hard and takes some time. Doing great things <u>requires</u> doing hard things. In the end, the changes required to dismantle silos will be worth it.

## 1) SHARE WEEKLY TEAM UPDATES ACROSS DEPARTMENTS

As part of our weekly cadence at Virtuous, each manager compiles a weekly email from their direct reports that outlines:

1. what each person accomplished last week and

2. what their primary focus is for the coming week.

Team leaders then combine the highlights from each of these emails into a single summarized email — and then share those summarized highlights with the entire team. The weekly summary emails help showcase progress, celebrate wins, create transparency, and share relevant insights.

To get a clearer picture of the value of this type of communication, let's put ourselves in the shoes of your Marketing/Communications Team. In this case, your Marketing team would receive weekly summary emails from Program, Ops, Volunteer, and Fundraising teams. Based on the insights shared in these emails, your Marketing would be better empowered to:

- Create more honest and compelling marketing materials based on the latest insights from Program.

- Align marketing messaging to upcoming Fundraising activities and better craft communications based on what

Fundraising is experiencing (e.g. "We need help with 1st to 2nd gift donor retention!").

- Understand the priority of IT and Ops initiatives, so that they have a better understanding of "why" a technology project is delayed and what workarounds are possible.

This process creates empathy, visibility, and accountability — but, more importantly, it surfaces opportunities where each team could benefit from working across departments to better solve organizational challenges. And, as strange as this sounds, it's likely that your more junior team members have no idea what happens in other departments. The visibility into the amazing work of your cause can create an increased sense of loyalty and purpose for team members who might otherwise feel isolated.

## 2) TRY JOB SHARING AND "DAY IN THE LIFE" EXERCISES

It's not always reasonable to ask someone on your team to do the job of a team member in another department for a day. That said, leading nonprofits are great at letting team members do "ride-alongs" with other departments to increase empathy and collaboration.

I recently talked with a nonprofit that works to prevent sex trafficking. This particular organization requires their fundraisers to spend time with field staff in Southeast Asia as they organize rescue missions for enslaved people. This simple exercise was transformative for the fundraisers that I spoke to. It allowed them to use firsthand experience and first-person language in their fundraising conversations — and created an entirely new level of empathy for the Program team.

Similarly, in the for-profit world, the popular shoe company Zappos required all early employees to work in Customer Support for two weeks before starting their new role. Even corporate attorneys were required to answer phones or support tickets from customers. This simple practice ensured that all Zappos employees had empathy for both the customer and the frontline Customer Support team. It also quickly eliminated any egos from the team. In the world of Zappos, if you're too good to talk to customers then you don't belong here!

To be clear, job sharing and ride-alongs require extra work from your team and organizational buy-in. But when done well, they can dramatically improve your organization's ability to cross team divides and accomplish common goals.

## 3) MAP THE CONSTITUENT JOURNEY WITH A FOCUS ON POTENTIAL GAPS

In our first book, I talked a lot about the importance of mapping your nonprofit's "Donor Journey." Journey mapping is simply a way to identify how different "constituent personas" experience your organization, moving from initial awareness to becoming a donor, volunteer, or loyal advocate for the cause.

While mapping the typical donor journey can be incredibly valuable, it's essential to recognize that your donors are whole people with different levels of involvement with your organization. Throughout their journey, each person will interact with the departments in your organization in different ways and for various reasons. Mapping the path of your constituents and identifying potential gaps they encounter in your organization will help ensure your departments provide a coherent experience.

In almost every nonprofit, there's a possibility that your constituents engage in ways other than donating (e.g. adopted a pet, visited your museum, attended your college, served at your food pantry, attended an event, received care, etc). Working with a cross-functional team to map all potential constituent touchpoints will inevitably create a better experience for your constituents. But it will also help your teams identify data gaps, collaboration gaps, or missing hand-offs that create poor experiences and inhibit generosity.

## CREATING A CULTURE OF TRANSPARENCY

We'll dig more into team culture in a later practice, but I wanted to touch on the cultural value of transparency here, as it has such a profound impact on collaboration. We all admire transparency when we encounter it in others. It's like a breath of fresh air. And when transparency is institutionalized within a nonprofit, it can create the organizational clarity needed to solve problems and drive innovation. But how do we create a culture of transparency within our teams and the organizations that we steward?

For a culture of transparency to flourish, nonprofit leadership should begin by modeling the following behaviors as they collaborate across teams:

1. Receive honest feedback with grace. Honest feedback is a gift!

2. Reward individuals who show up openly and share contrary opinions.

3. Practice humility by admitting failure.

4. Assume good intentions when receiving or giving hard feedback.

Cultures of transparency are marked by high trust and direct, honest feedback. Team members are provided with clear visibility into the direction and health of the organization. And, whenever possible, great organizations explain "why" they are moving in a particular direction.

Within transparent organizations, senior leaders often solicit critical feedback from individual contributors on the team without creating the fear of punishment or retribution. They model authentic honesty and quickly admit mistakes. In this context, individual contributors have a seat at the table. As a result, everyone on the team feels heard and respected, even if their suggestions aren't implemented.

The forward-thinking nonprofit Invisible Children embodied transparency by embracing the ideal "The Best Idea Wins." At Invisible Children, it didn't matter whether you were an executive or an intern — the organization's leadership facilitated an environment that embraced the collective team's unique perspectives and creative ideas. Amid some of their most challenging and uncertain moments, the input from individual contributors at Invisible Children resulted in many of their most impactful fundraising and awareness campaigns.

When an organization's leadership demonstrates unwavering trust, it inevitably breeds full buy-in and ownership from the team. But, transparency doesn't come naturally in most organizations. It requires intentionally fostering honesty, safety, and permission to fail. Eventually, every organization and every team member will fail, but in a culture of transparency, failures are addressed head-on, not through gossip and back-channel communication. And no failure is seen as "final." Instead, failures create learning moments and shared opportunities for growth.

Encouraging transparency, failure, and dissenting opinions requires a culture that rewards and models disruption. Innovative nonprofits admit mistakes and communicate with transparency from the top down. Honesty and humility are lived out and celebrated by the organization's senior leaders. Managers assume the best intentions of their team members and reward pushback against the status quo. And their team is allowed to show up as their authentic selves without fear of judgment for questioning the status quo.

In the words of acclaimed actress and writer Ilka Chase, "The only people who never fail are those who never try." Failing within an environment of trust is what creates learning and momentum. It's the only viable path to real innovation and change.

One of our favorite expressions of trust and transparency is encapsulated in the values of Stratasan, an innovative healthcare company in Nashville, TN. Stratasan has diligently built a culture of transparency and works hard to live out the values they've set. I've included Stratasan's company values below in full because they paint an incredible picture of how this type of culture could look within a nonprofit.

### *Everybody Makes the Coffee*

*We help where help is needed. Whether we're asked to pitch in to support a customer, run a meeting at the last minute, or make the morning coffee, everybody does what's necessary to keep the engine running. We don't believe in "pulling rank".*

### Our Success is My Success

*We support one another, strive for the success of the team, and recognize that nothing is done alone.*

### We'll Figure it Out

*We may not immediately have the answer to a question, but we're always committed to finding one. We believe most challenges are great opportunities to consciously show up, and with a resourceful attitude, brainstorm and consider the best course of action. Whatever comes our way, we won't quit until we find a solution.*

### Assume Positive Intent

*We start from the assumption that people are good and that their intentions are positive. We believe this builds stronger and more trusting relationships.*

### Honest Conversations Make Us Stronger

*Tough conversations, when approached with kindness and respect, yield the best outcomes for the business and the team. We don't shy away from difficult conversations. We approach them with curiosity and empathy, working to understand the other person's perspective prior to sharing our own.*

These values might look slightly different within your organization, but the overarching principles should be the same. Your battle cry should be, "We're all in this together. We provide honest transparent feedback. We trust our teammates. We assume good intent. And we lean in to listen and serve our team."

## RECOGNIZING POWER DYNAMICS

In most nonprofits, there is an inherent power structure that exists between senior leadership and individual team members. This power dynamic is accentuated when information is withheld or kept secret. If a senior leader knows important facts that the team doesn't, they are intrinsically in a position of power. This power dynamic can exist between individual members of your team and is amplified when it takes place within senior leadership.

When you take the power imbalance created when information is withheld and throw in the natural human desire to feel important, you have the perfect cocktail for unhealthy teams, burnout, gossip, and ineffectiveness.

Knowing this power dynamic exists to some degree in all organizations, how do nonprofits operate in a way that distributes power throughout the organization?

"Great leaders are vulnerable, open-minded, and supportive," Heather Hiscox says. "They recognize the destructive nature of command and control structures and they don't rely on hierarchy and power."

Bestselling author John C. Maxwell said it this way: "If you think you're leading, but no one is following, then you are only taking a walk." True leadership isn't about hoarding power or commanding respect. The best leaders serve their teams by freely giving away power.

To develop empathy and serve your team well, you must first focus on listening. Effective vulnerable leadership requires taking the time to understand the needs, desires, and superpowers of those around you.

Heather Hiscox had this to say about the most effective nonprofit leaders: "They will talk to volunteers and frontline staff, the people doing the work. They interact with the community and the internal stakeholders, recognize their value, and want to learn from them. They also understand the sticky place that managers occupy trying to meet the requirements and expectations of their bosses while keeping everyone below them informed and engaged. They create curious cultures, and at the end of the day, they're just trying to learn from everyone. Those are the leaders who succeed."

## CASE STUDY
### BETH FISHER AND MEL TROTTER MINISTRIES

Beth Fisher faced the daunting task of breaking down organizational silos and building a culture of transparency from scratch when she became the VP of Advancement at Mel Trotter Ministries. After 25 years in the corporate world, she entered the nonprofit sector and was baffled by the team silos that she encountered. She had inherited a team that was all too familiar with the revolving door of nonprofit staff turnover. Team members and managers cycled in and out, and those who stayed were getting very little done. To complicate the problem, there was very little collaboration or communication between departments throughout the organization.

Coming from a successful career in the corporate world, Beth wasn't accustomed to this kind of siloed approach to work. She was facing a big challenge, but she understood that her success in the role would be largely dependent on her ability to destroy team silos and increase transparency.

"Wherever you have people and wherever you have a mission, whether that's selling a product or affecting change in the world, you have to have a strategy," Beth says. "And strategy involves people."

Beth began working to increase transparency from day one. She gathered her entire team in person and aligned everyone around her role, her style, and her desire to drive results through better collaboration. She knew that in order to foster trust, she had to come from a place of brutal honesty and transparency. She was authentic and invited her team to provide honest feedback.

"I came in and said to the team, 'Here's why I'm here. Here's why I care, here's what we're here to do. Here's my backstory and here's how I operate.'"

To quickly understand the personalities and makeup of her team, she invited everyone to take an Enneagram test and share their results with each other. This exercise helped break down walls and create a better understanding of how each person operated. She took the time to meet with each team member individually to understand their personality, their personal goals, their role on the team, their style of working, and their connection to the organization and its larger mission.

"I began asking the tough questions. Where is this bus going? Are the people happy in the seats they occupy on this bus? What's the strategy here? At the same time, I was sharing myself with them. 'This is me,' I said. 'I'm not going to change after almost 50 years.

And nor do I expect you to change. But I do expect us to have an understanding about each other so that we can cultivate a mutual respect.'"

These exercises allowed everyone on the team to better understand one another and helped the team trust that Beth wanted the best for them and the broader mission. Because they understood Beth's unique personality, her team could say, "Oh, Beth's not talking a million miles a minute because she's yelling at me. She's talking like this because she's passionate." Conversely, Beth could understand, "You're not talking softly because you're lazy. You're reserved and calculating, thinking through several potential scenarios at once before you answer."

Another key practice Beth introduced was weekly stand-up meetings. Every Monday, Beth's team would huddle and answer the same questions: "What are you guys working on? What do you need help with? Where are you this week?"

Before Beth arrived, this regular cadence of internal communication wasn't happening. The team wasn't opposed to the increased collaboration, but it was never baked into their normal practices. Beth explained, "They just didn't have the right person on the bus at that time who understood organizational leadership, change, and structure."

For Mel Trotter, Beth was the catalyst for increased cross-team communication. She started bringing in the Communications and Development teams to join their weekly stand-up meetings. She set a clear structure for these short working meetings with the aim of open and productive communication across the teams.

"You've got five minutes on the clock," she would tell them. "We're not here to ramble. We're not going to go down the rabbit hole. Talk to us about donor problems. Tell us about what you have happening this week. Tell us where you need help."

Simply sitting down each week with team members from different teams fostered a sense of trust and camaraderie that had previously been absent. The functional teams began to get to know each other. They looked each other in the eye and listened to each other's pain points, successes, and obstacles. As a result, they were able to quickly find solutions to long-standing problems. Now, when problems are presented, each team feels empowered to craft an actionable plan with the full trust of the team. Everyone walks out of the stand-up meetings with an accurate picture of the top priorities for the week, and the people responsible for each task.

"It took me back a little bit," Beth admits. "I kept asking, 'Why isn't this happening?' Those conversations and that sort of execution didn't exist. But once we started that meeting, it became very clear who was adding value and where the gaps were. When we had a level of accountability and visibility, we could begin to rearrange our work to maximize the impact."

Within a couple of months, the other departments at Mel Trotter followed Beth's lead. Their executive leadership team changed drastically over the next few years. They flattened the organization, increased collaboration, and created a structure for scale. When Beth arrived, there were 16 people on the leadership team — today there are five. This streamlined structure allows for more transparency, communication, and cooperation between the different arms of the organization.

"Our departmental leaders meet on a monthly basis. The other teams on the programmatic side of the house began to see that structure breeds a lot more execution and change across the board. Now, when the leadership team meets, we have constructive meetings that stay on task. We're not having meetings just to meet. We're saying, 'What are you doing here? What can I do to help?'"

"I tell the team all the time, 'Clarity is kindness.' When I'm being clear about what I'm asking you to do, it's not to be mean. It's so we can collectively decide if this is the right task and the right role. My three words are hungry, humble, and smart. To me, two out of the three usually win and we can work on the third. I am interested in people, and trying to find the best place they fit into our larger organization."

Today, Mel Trotter's team leads from transparency, candor, and focused collaboration. They have seen dramatic improvements in their ability to fight homelessness in Grand Rapids over the past few years. Our team at Virtuous was given the opportunity to tour Mel Trotter's facilities and meet with their team, and we were blown away by their dedication to drive collaboration and innovation on behalf of their donors and the amazing people in the community that they serve.

Like with Mel Trotter, creating a transparent culture at your organization will be a process — and it will take time and intentional work. The lasting benefits are well worth it.

## GETTING PRACTICAL: SIMPLE PRACTICES TO INCREASE TRANSPARENT COLLABORATION

Breaking down team silos can seem like a daunting task. But the most significant positive changes are often the result of simple shifts in increasing transparency that create outsized downstream impact. Start by doing the easy things well, and don't get overwhelmed.

Here are a few small changes that we've seen have an outsized positive impact in increasing transparent collaboration and empowering your team:

- Reward and openly celebrate honest feedback across teams given with candor and grace. Get personal. Give your team specific examples of when you've personally received candid feedback and how it helped you get better. Admit your own failures, but don't shy away from being direct and clear with others. Examples and vulnerability provide a template for your team.

- Over-communicate any change in direction with your team. Big changes often need to be communicated four or five times to fully sink in.

- Practice active listening. Ask questions of your team and then re-state what you've heard to ensure everyone is on the same page. Prioritize relationships and acknowledge that everyone brings different experiences, knowledge, and superpowers to every conversation. Build trust by listening and valuing each person's perspective.

- Help your team and adjacent teams understand the "WHY" for decisions. Provide transparency around how the organization operates, what results are important, and how decisions get made. Invite questions and address concerns in a public forum when possible.

- <u>Share both wins and challenges across teams</u>. Don't sweep failures under the rug. Acknowledge them as opportunities to learn and grow

The heart of a thriving nonprofit is its people. Leading with transparency and creating a culture of trust allows your team to maximize its potential. When your team feels like they can trust their coworkers, leaders, and neighboring departments, the organization will be aligned to achieve its mission.

When transparency is modeled across your departments, you'll find that team silos begin to disintegrate. Authenticity breeds trust and collaboration. Great teams create alignment by sharing information freely, celebrating the wins of others, and admitting failures to accelerate learning.

## SUMMARY

I get it. Working in departmental silos often reduces headaches in the short term. Smaller teams can often make decisions faster, which creates a feeling of increased progress. As the saying goes, "the smaller the ship, the easier it is to steer."

But five small ships have a tendency to begin sailing in different directions, getting in each other's way and ultimately slowing down progress. As the gap widens, impact is inhibited, trust erodes, and teams become disillusioned.

Increasing impact over the long haul will require prioritizing collaboration, breaking down departmental walls, and empowering your team. Ensure everyone has access to the information they need to do their job and understand the broader mission. Admit failure, model transparency, and relentlessly dismantle walls between teams.

Intentional and aligned team collaboration is the recipe to take your nonprofit organization to the next level. The end result will be increased employee satisfaction, better donor/volunteer experiences, and the seeds of lasting innovation.

# METRICS AND QUARTERLY GOAL SETTING

*"If you aim at nothing, you will hit it every time."*
*– Zig Ziglar*

In the mid-2000s, YouTube began seeing significant traction in the burgeoning world of online video consumption. Internet speeds were increasing while more and more internet users were now seeing themselves as "content creators," not just content consumers. In October 2006, the team at Google recognized this growing trend and purchased YouTube for $1.65 billion.

While this purchase represented a big win for the scrappy team at YouTube, Google saw the acquisition as a MUCH bigger opportunity for growth. In 2012, Google executive Shishir Mehrotra decided to significantly up the ante. Rather than staying satisfied with slow, incremental growth, he decided to pursue the audacious goal of getting to 1 billion hours of YouTube video viewing time. Achieving this goal would require 10X growth for the YouTube platform over the course of four years. It would also mean that YouTube would functionally capture 20% of the world's TV watch time. If you grew up in the TV generation like I did, this goal would have seemed completely outrageous!

To hit their audacious new goal, Google enlisted the help of legendary VC John Doerr. Doerr's system of managing to Objectives and Key Results created a framework for Google to maniacally attack their goal, measure their progress, and prioritize their work. In the months leading up to their deadline, the Google team made a mind-blowing 150 incremental changes to the platform, with an average of .2% increase in viewing time per change. As a result, YouTube officially hit 1 billion hours of video view time two months ahead of schedule and became one of the most dominant forces on the modern internet.

## ALIGNING TO ORGANIZATIONAL GOALS

The story of YouTube's success may feel disconnected from the work at a typical nonprofit. With under-resourced teams and restricted annual budgets, 10X growth might feel like an unattainable dream. That said, I think there are several lessons that we can draw from YouTube's success that could have a direct impact on the success and scale of your organization.

Our first practice focused largely on removing silos within your organization and creating a culture of collaboration to drive your organization forward. In other words, we focused on answering the question, "How should the organization be structured to drive success?" In Practice 2, we'll shift our focus to the question of,

"What goals should we pursue, and how do we align our team around hitting audacious goals?"

Orienting your team around a singular audacious goal requires intentional discipline and clear communication. Even when data and team silos are dismantled, it still takes conscious, consistent effort to get everyone on your team moving toward a shared goal and aligned vision of the future. But, when your team can focus on a specific goal, outsized results are possible. Like Google and YouTube, a goal-aligned team can move quickly and autonomously to prioritize and execute on the more impactful work.

The good news is that aligning a nonprofit team around a shared vision is typically easier than aligning a for-profit team around a shared vision. Nonprofit organizations are mission-focused by nature and are already committed to solving a big problem in the world. In most cases, your team has already bought into the organization's mission, and everyone is clear on the overarching goal.

The real work for nonprofits lies in breaking your long-term vision into achievable quarterly goals and trackable steps along the way. In many nonprofits, short-term goals are often fuzzy and don't connect directly to the daily work of each team member — or they are too far out into the future. At Virtuous, we say that every team member should "know their number." For our team, this means that everyone should clearly understand the metric that they are individually responsible for. And they should see how their work directly impacts our organizational metrics and quarterly goals. This approach helps create tremendous clarity for our team and drives meaningful purpose in each individual's work.

In many cases, silos between teams contribute to the problem of ineffective goal setting. I've worked with nonprofits that allow each team to set their own goals with little collaboration across the organization. Unlike with YouTube, the individual teams at these organizations are not aiming at a singular north star. As a result, team members cannot make minor corrections along the way and have confidence that each change is helping move the team closer to the ultimate outcome.

In addition, I've seen situations where each team is tracking their progress toward a goal in a different system. The Fundraising team tracks dollars raised in a CRM, while the Volunteer team monitors the number of participants that signed up in their volunteer management platform, and so on. In these organizations, no single team has a clear view of how their work impacts the metrics of other teams or the overall results across the organization.

In order to correct these problems, leading nonprofits have implemented clear frameworks for tracking goals and key outcomes across their organization. Rather than pursuing isolated, team-specific metrics, healthy organizations roll up team KPIs (Key Performance Indicators) that contribute to a shared set of organizational goals. In this model, each team member understands how their work impacts not only their specific team but also the organization as a whole.

In a perfect world, most organizational goals would be shared by multiple teams. For example, the Volunteer team would own a portion of the fundraising goal, while the Fundraising team would be responsible for surfacing potential volunteers or advocates to help meet the Volunteer team's goals. I've even worked with nonprofits where the Program team is held accountable for calling volunteers and donors every month while the Operations and Finance teams make decisions based on specific fundraising or program goals.

In this model, challenges in one department become opportunities for other departments to lean in and help. Each team is responsible for the entire organization's success, and they are all aware of how their tasks support each other and the nonprofit's main focus areas.

## GOAL-SETTING FRAMEWORKS

Most successful organizations drive KPI alignment by using a common goal-setting framework. Two of our favorite frameworks are OKRs (Objectives and Key Results) and Rocks (EOS Framework — aka the Entrepreneur Operating System). If you're unfamiliar with these systems, we highly recommend the books, *Measure What Matters* by John Doerr (OKRs) and *Traction* by Gino Wickman (EOS), both of which are excellent organizational resources that I have used personally at my organization and the nonprofits that I've worked with.

In both the OKR and EOS frameworks, the leadership team should work together to create shared goals across multiple teams (Program Outcomes, Volunteerism, Activism, Financial Giving, Retention, Sustainability, Constituent Engagement, etc). After goals are set, each team should participate in quarterly and annual planning to ensure every team member knows how their daily job and individual KPIs impact the overarching organizational goals.

We'll provide a brief overview of each framework, but we encourage you to do more research to determine what works best for your organization.

## Objectives and Key Results (OKRs)

In the OKR framework, each team aligns around key objectives that are both lofty and measurable. The objectives are made public to the entire organization, and teams are regularly evaluated based on their progress towards their objectives.

Most organizations set longer-term OKRs (1-3 years) along with quarterly OKRs that help track shorter-term milestones toward larger goals. Each OKR includes a single Objective (what we want to achieve) and 2-4 Key Results (what we want to accomplish/measure to achieve the objective). The team at What Matters defines OKRs this way[1]:

### Objectives

*An Objective is simply what is to be achieved, no more and no less. By definition, Objectives are significant, concrete, action oriented, and (ideally) inspirational. When properly designed and deployed, they're a vaccine against fuzzy thinking and ineffective execution.*

### Key Results

*Key Results benchmark and monitor how we get to the Objective. Effective KRs are specific, time-bound, and aggressive yet realistic. Most of all, they are measurable and verifiable. You either meet a Key*

---

1    Ryan Panchadsaram, "What is an OKR? Definition and Examples," What Matters, https://www.whatmatters.com/faqs/okr-meaning-definition-example#

*Result's requirements or you don't — there is no gray area, no room for doubt. At the end of the designated period, typically a quarter, we do a regular check and grade the Key Results as fulfilled or not. Where an Objective can be long lived, rolled over for a year or longer, Key Results evolve as the work progresses. Once they are all completed, the Objective is achieved.*

Because these objectives can be inherently ambitious, employees aren't penalized for falling short. In fact, most great organizations only hit their OKRs about 70% of the time. Instead, these objectives are intended to motivate and inspire teams to achieve more than they previously thought possible and get outside of their comfort zone to do so.

To help put a bit more meat on the bone, I'll provide a sample OKR that might exist within a Fundraising team.

Objective: Launch a planned giving program to create future organizational resiliency.

- KR1: Engage with 500 potential planned givers
- KR2: Formalize relationship with planned gift attorney and launch infrastructure required to support gifts
- KR3: Receive initial commitments from 30 people for planned gifts totaling $1 million in future giving

In this case, our "Planned Giving" OKR might represent one of the three core OKRs for the entire Fundraising team this quarter. The OKR would have a single team member who was ultimately responsible for the success of this OKR. In addition, the OKR results (e.g. $1 million in future giving) would roll up to a broader organizational or fundraising OKR related to financial resiliency and sustainability.

Generally speaking, your organization shouldn't set more than 3-5 OKRs per quarter. If you haven't used this type of framework in the past, then I'd recommend starting with three. Limiting your objectives will help your team focus on the most important metrics and areas of most significant impact.

After establishing organization-wide OKRs, each team should craft 3-5 OKRs that ladder up to the overarching organizational objectives. If it's unclear how a team-level OKR contributes directly to an organizational OKR, then it probably shouldn't be on the list. Or, in some cases, if team-level OKRs are misaligned, then the top-level organizational objective needs to be modified based on feedback from the individual teams.

Typically, team-level OKRs are planned and confirmed during a quarterly planning process. Team planning helps each team create a plan to attack each OKR while building team-wide buy-in and collaboration. At the end of the quarterly planning process, each team member should clearly understand how their work contributes directly to a key result and what metrics they are personally responsible for. OKRs provide each team with clarity on the results they must achieve while allowing for maximum flexibility on how they get there.

I've seen this model create massive amounts of clarity and improved results in organizations of all sizes. Google, Intel, and countless others have leveraged OKRs to quickly align their teams around audacious goals (including the YouTube team!). And many of the most forward-thinking nonprofit leaders have dramatically accelerated program impact, fundraising results, and team member engagement using the OKR model.

## SMART Rocks Using the EOS Framework

The EOS/Rock framework is very similar to the OKR framework in that it helps leaders prioritize tasks and projects over a 90-day period. The "Rock" concept is part of the more extensive Entrepreneurial Operating System (EOS) framework. In the EOS framework, an organization's leadership team works to establish a clear and measurable 3-year vision for the future. The executive team and department leaders then work backwards from the 3-year vision to create more detailed 1-year and 90-day plans.

In the EOS system, the leadership team chooses the 3-7 of the most important measurable outcomes ("Rocks") they want to achieve in the next 90 days. These outcomes should be moving them toward their larger 1- and 3-year goals, and every team member should be doing focused work over the 90-day time period to impact their Rocks.

Like in the OKR framework, teams plan their Rocks on a quarterly basis to ensure each Rock will have the highest impact on the organization's long-term objectives. Rock planning should create team buy-in, clarity around goals, and increased alignment with the organizational vision.

In some ways, the EOS system provides a simpler approach to goal management than OKRs. It also leverages a helpful tool called a Vision/Traction Organizer (VTO) to organize your 3-year plan and force organizational clarity around your long-term goals and organizational mission.

A few additional advantages of EOS include its structured recommendations for meeting cadences, problem-solving tools, and team design. In some ways, EOS might feel more constricting and prescriptive than other frameworks, but when implemented well, I've seen it effectively align and accelerate countless nonprofits.

If you want to dig into the EOS Framework, the best place to start is the book *Traction* by Gino Wickman. Even if you are already effectively setting goals, *Traction* can be an invaluable resource to structure your team for success.

Both OKRs and Rocks are fantastic organizational frameworks for aligning on key objectives and goals. They also provide regular checkpoints for individual employees, teams, and the organization as a whole. I would encourage you to investigate both the OKR and EOS models to determine what works best for your organization. You may already have a clear goal-setting framework in place, but there will likely be learnings from each framework that can help align your teams and drive measurable results.

## SMART GOALS

No matter what goal framework you choose to use, every organization would benefit from formatting its goals using the *SMART* method. SMART goals certainly aren't a new concept, and you're likely already familiar with the SMART approach. That said, it's always helpful to review what a "good" goal looks like before you adopt a new goal-setting process.

When leaders sit down to set their team goals, or when managers meet with employees to set individual goals, they should make sure all goals are:

- "S" – Specific – What specific outcome do you want to achieve? What specifically needs to be done? What is the "number" that indicates success?

- "M" – Measurable – What data or reports will be used to measure progress toward the goal?

- "A" – Achievable – Is this goal realistically achievable for your organization within the time constraints? As a side note, you are going for "achievable but hard." Anything worth doing carries the risk of failure!

- "R" – Relevant – Does this help achieve our broader organizational goals? What are the opportunity costs of not doing something else?

- "T" – Time-Bound – What is the completion date? Who on your team is accountable to that date?

As much as possible, avoid creating goals around a project or task (e.g. launch a new website). Instead, try to orient goals around the ultimate outcome (e.g. increase web traffic and engagement by 20%). Aligning to outcomes helps your entire team focus on your ultimate organizational goals, providing room for creativity in how those outcomes are achieved. This approach gives more ownership and empowerment to the team members working on the projects to hit the goal and the autonomy to creatively achieve results.

## INITIAL GOAL SETTING

For many nonprofits, your team may have never implemented formal goal-setting sessions. In that case, this is an excellent opportunity to gather your team and get everyone on the same page regarding your organization's top priorities.

We encourage leaders to set aside a four-hour facilitated planning session every quarter to create alignment and reset metrics. These sessions are a good opportunity to monitor progress towards specific objectives, but they can also be a tremendous opportunity for team building, collaboration, and transparency.

Every organization is different, but we like to conduct these planning meetings offsite whenever possible. We also love including a meal or fun activity to help get the team out of their daily routine. We have seen time and time again that this simple equation produces great results:

a change of place + a change of pace for our teams = renewed clarity and vision

Planning meeting agendas can vary, but we would encourage you to include the following as a bare minimum:

- Review last quarter's results — how did we do? Be honest here! Failure is okay; sugar coating isn't!

- Share any learnings about what we should do differently.

- Review how goals need to shift based on broader organizational goals. Do we need to keep, kill, or combine any initiatives or goals?

- Outline any new initiatives for the coming quarter.

- Document your new goals for the coming quarter.

- Assign accountability for each goal. Who is the owner? Who needs to be consulted? Who should be informed on progress?

These goal-setting sessions are effective for both the leadership and individual team members to assess their KPIs and determine how they roll up into those larger objectives.

Once quarterly goals are set, they are shared broadly across the entire organization so that each team understands the main objectives for that quarter and how they can support other teams in reaching those objectives.

## MANAGING TO GOALS

Another problem we often encounter with nonprofit goal-setting is the "set it and forget" mindset. Many organizations create goals because they think they have to. Goals are set as an obligatory exercise without any real accountability or understanding of how to monitor progress. This is why the "Measurable" component of a SMART goal is so critical. If your team isn't committed to consistently tracking metrics and creating accountability for progress, you might as well not set any goals at all.

Managers or team leads are responsible for ensuring each team member is focused on their goals and progressing in the right direction. The process of managing to goals can vary across teams and be highly individualized. But it's important that you find a process that works for your team.

The organizations that we've worked with that have seen success follow a few common practices:

- Review metrics and progress toward goals in weekly one-on-one meetings and weekly status update emails.

- Mark goals as Red, Yellow, or Green each week so the team can see what's on track, what's in danger, and what's falling behind. This color-coding system can also be displayed on monitors throughout the office for specific goals the organization wants the entire team to rally around.

- Leverage goal-tracking software or even Google Sheets to share goals with the entire organization — and then post weekly reminders with links to the goals in Slack or email.

- Establish monthly "Status" meetings with the entire department or team (depending on organizational size) to check in on goal progress. Breaking the quarterly goals into bite-sized check-ins every four weeks keeps the group on track with the goals top of mind.

This level of goal transparency creates both team alignment and accountability around a metrics-driven approach to organizational success. Transparency is essential in consistently achieving hard goals. The more everyone knows, the more accountability there is — and the shared insights across departments breed increased teamwork and collaboration.

## CASE STUDY
### JUSTIN NARDUCCI AND CURE INTERNATIONAL

Justin Narducci is the President/CEO of CURE International, a global Christian nonprofit organization that owns and operates a network of charitable children's hospitals around the world. In his 15+ years working in nonprofit leadership, Narducci has learned how critical mission alignment is to organizational success.

"I think one of the biggest things that people want to know is, where are we going?" Narducci says. "And there are a lot of different ways to identify where you're going. You could be like Moses, coming down from the mountaintop and saying, 'The Lord told me we're going here.' People do that all the time. They make the decision and then tell everyone else what to do, and the whole plan comes from this one person. But we took a different approach."

When Narducci took over leadership of CURE International, he inherited an organization that had been operating with a consistent set of practices for over 25 years. He was, for all intents and purposes, an outsider. And, though he had extensive experience leading and innovating within nonprofits, he wasn't in a position to make wholesale organizational changes without bringing the team along. Instead, his mission was to begin aligning the team around clear goals based on intentional learning and research.

"We started with guided listening exercises," Narducci explains. "For the first six months, we asked people what was working, what wasn't working, and where they would like to see this ministry in five years. We asked over 50 people these questions, people who worked in different functions and at different levels within the organization. Then we synthesized those answers, looking for commonalities and identifying key areas of concern. We listened and learned and most importantly, we didn't try to solve any problems right away. It was a slow burn at the beginning as we began to identify what was mission critical and what wasn't."

This listening exercise was time-consuming, but it gave Narducci critical insight into the organization and its people that he needed to begin laying the groundwork for CURE's future.

"Next, we put a framework together to guide where we were going and how we were going to get there. We utilized the commonalities and trends that we heard in our listening sessions and took input from all those people to decide what that strategic plan would look like. We identified five to six key areas within the organization that needed to improve and made those our primary focus.

"One of the biggest questions we needed to answer right away was, who is our primary client? And that was a big deal because a lot of nonprofits try to serve everybody. But what ends up happening is that they serve a lot of people just okay, and don't really go above and beyond to change lives or provide exceptional service. So we went back to the question, who does the mission exist to serve? And you end up having to make some very hard decisions when you focus on things like that. You have to choose between clients who bring in much-needed dollars and the people in need that you're trying to help. You have to choose between different populations that need help — for us, it was a choice between adults and children. In the end, we decided to say that this mission exists for poor children and particularly for poor children who have disabilities."

For Narducci, aligning on this singular focus was the first and most important step to orienting the team around a larger organizational strategy.

"We have 1,110 employees. If nobody knows whom we're serving, then how can we be expected to make any real difference? So we brought everyone together and said, 'Look, this is whom we serve. So if you're doing something that doesn't serve this population, we need to phase it out. And that's what we're going to do over this strategic planning period. We're going to phase it out, and see how many more kids we can serve.'"

With that purpose in mind, Narducci and his team began crafting a strategic plan. It wasn't just enough to pursue their greater purpose in fuzzy, generalized terms. They needed to know what specific changes would need to be made to effectively serve more kids.

The strategic plan looked at a wide variety of organizational systems, from facility improvements to ministry outreach, doctor recruitment, and new service lines. At each stage, they encountered new roadblocks, new questions, and new pockets of resistance. But they continued to recalibrate their team to the primary goal of serving more children — and then allowed that goal to guide all decision-making.

But, for Justin and his team, creating the plan was the easy part. Bringing everyone else on board and creating organization-wide buy-in was much harder.

"Suddenly, it was like, hey, we have this glossy brochure of a plan… now how do we make it happen at the grassroots level?"

Narducci's team turned to the EOS Model and began implementing the Rocks goal framework to break down their strategic plan into actionable pieces for every individual team and team member. And it all started at the top.

"Our leadership team consists of four people. These are all trusted CURE folks who have been promoted from within. We came together for two days and mapped out our strategic plan over the next three years. Then, we meet every year for an annual offsite where we plan that year's annual goals. Then we conduct weekly meetings every Tuesday where we review KPIs and put together quarterly status updates and make sure we're trending towards our annual goals and dealing with issues that come up across the team. It makes us incredibly efficient because there's a mechanism in place to resolve problems. If something's not working, we tell people to raise it with their manager. We meet every week and we're going to talk about it, and at least try to resolve it instead of getting stuck."

It didn't take long for Narducci's strategic plan to start producing results.

"When you get into that rhythm with competent people, things start happening. We started to have a few small wins. For example, one of our focus areas was on medical equipment. Every hospital had different equipment. Some were old and crappy and some were new and shiny. We couldn't repair or support it all, so we created a new equipment list. We asked what hospitals liked and didn't like. We gave them a chance to tell us what they wanted and then created a universal list of equipment. Then, we started rolling out the list of equipment at every hospital. Everyone started getting the tools they needed to be successful.

"That's really what the role of the executive is, I think," Narducci says. "To provide the overall direction and help people get the tools they need to be successful in their roles."

## SUMMARY

As a nonprofit leader, you can choose a goal-setting framework or process that works best for your organization. But, to be successful, your goal-setting activities should always include:

1. Aligning your goals and outcomes across all teams, not just one department or team.

2. Using data to closely measure and manage the progress you want to see.

3. Ensuring everyone on the team "knows their number" and understands how they contribute to the organization's success.

4. Creating clear ownership, timelines, and short loops of accountability to keep everyone on track.

The more organizational muscle you can build in these four key areas, the more effective you'll be in driving increased impact and generosity.

# THE AGILE NONPROFIT

*"Learn from yesterday, live for today, hope for tomorrow.*
*The important thing is not to stop questioning."*
*– Albert Einstein*

In early 2022, I found myself in a meeting with a group of exceptional nonprofit professionals. We were there to re-engage with the local nonprofit community after being stuck at home for a year and to dissect our learnings from the pandemic.

As we discussed the rapid upheaval caused by COVID, one local nonprofit leader blurted out, "I've never heard the word 'pivot' so many times in my entire life!" Her statement received a few chuckles from the other leaders in the room, but her underlying sentiment resonated with me. During the pandemic, nonprofits were forced into an overwhelming amount of change. Rather than planning their activities for the entire year, the nonprofit leaders in the room had to meet DAILY to re-evaluate their program and fundraising tactics. And in many cases, entire teams were repurposed to take on completely new and unknown challenges. The pace of change was unprecedented, and it left many nonprofit leaders on the brink of burnout.

Throughout the chaos of 2020-2021, it became clear that many nonprofit leaders didn't have the tools necessary to adapt and change quickly. But, whether they were prepared or not, nonprofits were forced to "pivot" at a breakneck speed in order to survive. Unfortunately, many of the changes nonprofits made during COVID felt unstructured, disorganized, and ineffective. And nonprofit teams felt the whiplash from constant strategic "pivots" within an organization. Balls were dropped. Results weren't effectively measured. And, in some sense, it felt like many nonprofits were driving in the dark with little confidence that their work would achieve the desired outcome.

The reality is that COVID was simply an accelerated microcosm of the world we now live in. The pandemic magnified these challenges, but the problem is not new. For the past decade, many nonprofits have struggled to adapt to the increasing pace of change in the world around them.

Those who know me know that I'm a huge soccer fan. I'm happy to watch soccer any time and at any level, whether it's my beloved Chelsea in the English Premier League or my nine-year-old daughter's recreational soccer team. And if you've been around soccer for as long as I have, you understand the critical importance of the term "pace of play." In other words, as the level of competition grows in soccer, so does the velocity of each player's decision-making and speed.

Occasionally, you'll see an inexperienced soccer player unaccustomed to the pace of play at a particular level. While other players on the field seem to effortlessly pass the ball around and predict how the game is progressing, the slower player is left spinning in circles, perpetually two steps behind. The less mature players desperately want to impact the game, but by the time they arrive at the ball, the play has long since passed them by.

Often, nonprofit professionals can feel like soccer players who have advanced to a level beyond their ability. They desperately try to adapt to their changing environment, but feel like they are changing too slowly and arriving at the proverbial ball too late.

But there's good news. All hope is not lost. Keeping up with the pace of play in our modern world IS possible. But, becoming more agile and effective in the face of change will require a new set of tools and processes. It will mean moving beyond the status quo and adopting new ways of working designed for the increasing pace of your cause.

## ORGANIZATIONAL BARRIERS TO CHANGE

The reality is that we live in a world of constant change. I started this book by mentioning Martec's Law, which shows how the increasing speed of technological advancements makes it nearly impossible to keep up, let alone pull ahead. The nonprofit world, in particular, has struggled to keep pace with societal and technological changes. And a growing disconnect between nonprofits and their communities has driven hundreds of well-meaning organizations into irrelevance.

I can't tell you the number of times I've worked with nonprofits that are unwilling to try new ideas based on an often irrational fear of disrupting the status quo at their organization. Rather than considering a new idea as a "hypothesis" to be tested, traditional nonprofit leaders often treat every new idea as a potential threat to the ordinary course of business. As a result, the status quo persists — and innovation dies on the vine.

Many of the nonprofits we've worked with over the past decade have struggled to adapt to change for various reasons. First, most nonprofits live and die by annual budget cycles that lock down team expenses and hiring for the year. Team leaders set budgets once a year, typically in June or December, and then focus most of their energy on the predetermined activities approved in the budget. Because these budgets are often inflexible and don't carve out time or money for new ideas, organizations miss out on new opportunities to adapt on the fly. Functionally, in budget-cycle-driven nonprofits new ideas can only be introduced once a year, making it almost impossible for nonprofits to learn, adapt, or respond to new opportunities in real time. And, in the worst cases, annual budget cycles can create a perverse disincentive to cut ineffective programs because of the perception that unused money will be lost.

In many cases, executive leaders within these organizations may recognize that particular initiatives from the annual plan need to be revised as the year progresses. And because there is no clear mechanism to pivot priorities, some leaders resort to constantly introducing "new ideas" without a means to modify the existing budget to cut unproductive work.

Within these organizations, teams experience "new idea overload" from leadership. They feel like they are constantly thrown into a new project that is above and beyond the existing plan and ultimately doomed to fail. As a result, most nonprofits build up a cultural resistance to change over time.

To move past traditional models and truly innovate, nonprofits need a better framework for testing new ideas and managing change. They need an operating model that allows them to test ideas in a low-risk environment, learn over time, quickly pivot away from non-performing ideas, and build organizational buy-in along the way.

## AGILE TO THE RESCUE

If you haven't spent much time around growing tech companies, you may be unfamiliar with the Agile methodology as it applies to businesses and nonprofits. At their core, Agile principles are designed to help teams pivot quickly and increase their "pace of play." Rather than experiencing burnout and misalignment during seasons of change, Agile teams can adapt quickly, align to measurable results, and take advantage of new opportunities.

To help achieve these goals, the Agile methodology provides a framework for teams to perform short work cycles with high transparency and accountability. Team activities are planned within two-week "sprints," and the planning process for each sprint allows teams to learn on the fly, evaluate their progress, and pivot in real time. Larger projects are divided into bite-sized chunks that integrate stakeholder feedback and deliver provable value along the way. Unlike traditional project management processes, the Agile approach allows nonprofits to adapt and respond quickly to changes in their organization or community... while minimizing the burnout typically associated with change.

Adopting this approach will require many nonprofits to rethink how they get work done, and how they think about fixed annual budgets based on pre-planned projects. But, in the end, adopting Agile will also result in more effective teams who perpetually learn and refocus on the highest value work for the cause.

When discussing Agile, I often cite the somewhat overused example of charting a course on a boat. If a boat captain sets sail across the Atlantic, but is just a couple of degrees off, the boat is likely to land in Morocco instead of England. Successful navigation means consistently evaluating your current position and realigning your course to your ultimate goal. In the same way, the Agile methodology creates discipline in measuring progress and consistently realigning teams to work with the most significant impact.

In addition to continuous realignment, Agile provides a mechanism for quickly adapting to changes in the world around you. Mike Tyson famously said, "Everyone has a plan until you get punched in the face." For many nonprofits, those external "punches" sometimes feel like they are flying in with unfair and unrelenting frequency. The Agile methodology is not only designed to block punches from the external environment (punches like pandemics, economic downturns, policy changes, etc.) but also to respond quickly with innovative counter-punches in response to new opportunities.

## A HYPOTHETICAL EXAMPLE

Let's look at a practical example to better understand the power of the Agile approach. Imagine that your nonprofit works with underserved families in your community. Your leadership team meets in January to set your goals for the year. The budget is divvied up between teams and projects, and everyone on your team knows their priorities for the year.

Then, in February, a sudden disaster in the community creates an urgent and unplanned need. Your frontline team working with the community has some ideas for how they might help, but in the fog of chaos, the right path forward is unclear. In this scenario, nonprofits typically pursue one of three common approaches.

The first approach would be to do nothing. Your organization is locked into its approved plan, and it seems too risky to upset the status quo. As a result, you simply ignore the changing needs of the community and charge ahead as planned. While you might hit the budget, you limit your impact while eroding trust from your community and team.

The second approach would be to adapt to the needs of the community by re-planning and re-budgeting the entire year. New annual plans are created, and team members are permanently re-allocated. And, after a month or two of trying to turn the Titanic, you begin responding to the new needs in your community. In the worst-case scenario, the window of need passes or changes, and you are forced to re-plan again.

The third approach is to go rogue and throw the plan out the window. Team members are encouraged to do their best to serve the community in the moment, and everyone begins to do what they can with little regard to an overarching goal. Learnings are never shared across the team. Toes are stepped on. Work is duplicated. And chaos ensues.

The Agile methodology creates a fourth and more viable option to respond to changing needs. When teams adopt Agile, they have a framework for working quickly and evolving in real time. Agile gives your team permission to say, "We don't yet know what will be required to solve this problem, but we DO know how to jump in and learn quickly as we go."

I chose an illustration centered around "changing community needs" because it felt particularly relevant given the stress placed on Program teams during COVID. That said, I could have provided any number of similar examples from the perspective of the Fundraising team. For most nonprofits, "annual planning" is at the heart of their fundraising programs. While annual planning around fundraising goals is essential, many Fundraising and Marketing teams aren't empowered to change course quickly as they learn throughout the year. Rather than fostering a culture of constant testing and adjustments, Fundraising teams often simply execute the prescribed plan and let the chips fall where they may.

Admittedly, there are already hundreds of organizations that have embraced this mindset. Many nonprofits I've worked with are well-equipped to quickly iterate and learn based on changing needs. Though many nonprofit leaders might not call their approach "Agile," they've already built a strong culture and operating model that allows them to pivot quickly. The Agile methodology simply provides clear language, mindsets, and processes around this approach that helps nonprofit teams bake agility into their DNA.

## HOW AGILE WORKS

Many of the world's most innovative companies use some form of the Agile methodology to manage their product development and marketing teams. Agile is a powerful tool because it not only promotes creativity and innovation but also utilizes a set framework meant to help teams act on new ideas quickly as they learn.

We'll dive into the specifics of each of these practices below. But, in short, the seven key components of Agile include:

1. Doing work as a team in short two-week intervals known as "**sprints.**"

2. Creating **small agile teams** around projects to increase collaboration and remove bureaucracy during sprints.

3. Assigning work in each sprint based on **small, measurable tasks**. When possible, each task in a sprint should be linked to a key organizational goal or specific information you'd like to learn. Every task should have a provable outcome and an owner.

4. Focusing on creating a "**Minimum Viable Product**" (MVP) in as few sprints as possible. An MVP should allow you to gather quick feedback and learnings from key stakeholders.

5. Reviewing your work product as a team at the end of each sprint to **provide feedback and create accountability.**

6. Using **retrospective meetings** at the end of each sprint to share key learnings over the past two weeks — and then make adjustments on the fly.

7. Leveraging **daily stand-ups and highly collaborative working environments** to quickly remove speed bumps during sprints.

We've seen nonprofits adopt this framework to better drive predictable outcomes, faster results, and accountability within each team or department. The Agile methodology provides nonprofits with a mechanism to adapt quickly — without devolving into "Wild West" chaos where team members aren't riding in the same direction toward a common goal.

We've often seen the Agile approach provide the greatest amount of leverage within nonprofit Marketing and Direct Response teams. Rather than planning and executing campaigns over the course of months with little visibility into results, Marketing teams experiment in short intervals with emails, social media ads, or smaller events. The learnings and response rates are shared during the next sprint planning meeting, and then the team iterates on each new idea to optimize performance. While the quarterly revenue goals for marketing should be predetermined, the team is given the flexibility to determine "how" the goal is achieved with consistent experimentation and optimization.

In the same way, Program teams who have embraced Agile can use two-week sprints to better respond to a crisis, or quickly test new program offerings. Rather than waiting for months to see if a new program change is successful, agile teams can quickly refine the best ideas and even more quickly cut the offerings that don't deliver the desired impact.

Mark Miller is the Founder and CEO of Historic, a nonprofit change agency. Historic helps nonprofits design and scale their branding to reach a wider audience. In his work, Miller straddles the worlds of technology, branding, and nonprofit innovation. And, to magnify the impact of Historic's work within nonprofits, Mark has fully embraced the Agile methodology.

"We structure a process that results in a Minimum Viable Product to test within days," Miller explains. "And that is such a foreign way of thinking for nonprofits. They get stuck on problems, and use their existing structures and systems to fix that problem, and it doesn't work, because they're using the same methodology that got them to the problem in the first place."

Miller emphasizes that the most agile nonprofits are the ones who will be able to best adapt to technological changes.

"The nonprofits that are going to stay relevant and the ones that are going to be able to raise more money, the ones that are going to grow and impact, are the ones that are going to be able to adapt to change faster and take advantage of those opportunities. And sometimes those opportunities look very, very different from traditional models."

But Miller knows that adapting to new opportunities can be one of the biggest challenges for nonprofits.

"Any time our clients tell us something can't be done or that 'this is the way it's always been done,' we immediately go and research if that's true. Often, we *can* do things a different way, and we discover potential new solutions through research and testing."

"We realized you have to adopt a better process and think creatively to do things differently. But it is possible, and that's how we do it now. It's radically different, but our clients love it because they own the process more deeply and they're more involved."

The team at Historic clearly understands that real change in the nonprofit space requires adaptability. The most effective teams will relentlessly introduce and test new solutions — and then pivot in real time based on what works. And, through this process, nonprofits will maniacally break through the status quo and accelerate innovation.

## STARTING WITH A GOAL

The key to effectively implementing Agile is to start with a clear set of goals based on measurable outcomes. The magic of Agile happens when you provide your team with a clear view of the destination but then allow for flexibility and creativity in how they get there.

Once you have your north-star vision defined, you can identify the necessary tasks and deliverables within each Agile sprint that maximizes your time to value. Every new idea or learning introduced during the Agile process should have the potential to move the organization closer to a defined, measurable outcome. In many cases, new ideas may fail, but Agile gives your team permission to quit working on non-performing ideas quickly based on the idea's inability to achieve a clear goal.

Starting with a goal-based approach can also help transcend the typical constraints associated with annual budgets. Rather than planning budgets around a set of "projects" to be accomplished, annual budgets can be reoriented around goals. For example, rather than specifying that your organization needs to hire a new digital marker to run social media and revamp your website, you might instead say, "We believe a digital marketer can add 1,000 new donors through digital channels." The Marketing team would then be allowed to test new ideas and pivot the tasks of the new team member based on the best way to accomplish the goal.

## ROLLING OUT AGILE AT YOUR ORGANIZATION

No two organizations are exactly the same, and your organization's implementation of Agile may vary based on your specific needs. That said, we recommend the following core tenets of the Agile methodology for most nonprofit teams.

While Agile can be useful for every team in your organization, we recommend starting with your Marketing/Communications or Fundraising departments. These teams, in particular, are often in the best position to create quick wins by embracing a more agile mindset.

## SPRINT PLANNING

Sprint Planning meetings provide a structured mechanism to help your team plan work for the next two-week period. It's often helpful to schedule a more extended 3- to 4-hour Sprint Planning meeting to kick off a new project. This longer format will create space to align your team around goals, assign team ownership, and discuss the problems that you're trying to solve. After the initial kickoff meeting, it's typically sufficient to reduce Sprint Planning time to two hours once every two weeks.

Most Agile advocates recommend restricting your Agile team size to 5-11 people. The Agile community lovingly refers to this structure as a "pizza box size" team because it's small enough to feed the entire team with an extra large pepperoni pizza. Pizza box teams provide enough horsepower to collaborate and do significant work while avoiding the bureaucracy and complexity of larger teams.

During Sprint Planning, your team gathers around a whiteboard or a shared collaboration tool (Google Docs and Trello are a great place to start). Every team member participates in the meeting while the project owner documents the next steps and ensures that the team doesn't get trapped in long rabbit holes.

The result of Sprint Planning should be a clear work plan for the next two weeks with specific tasks assigned to each team member.

The Sprint Planning process should also actively encourage input from key stakeholders outside the team. At Virtuous, we often include key members from other teams in Sprint Planning who will receive the benefit of the work performed during the sprint. Individual team members are allowed to ask probing questions and test assumptions in real time to ensure that our work will actually fulfill its purpose.

For example, if your Marketing team is doing a creative piece to talk about the impact of one of your programs, then you should have someone from the Program team in the room during Sprint Planning to provide feedback. Or, if your Fundraising team is planning a new campaign for the quarter, they should include team members from the Marketing and Volunteer teams to ensure the timing and messaging for all communications are aligned.

Each Sprint Planning meeting should start with a quick review of the previous sprint. Every team member should be given the opportunity to show their work from the previous sprint and share any learnings. These reviews help increase accountability, readjust the project's pace, and allow for changes based on learnings.

After the team has shared their work from the previous sprint, the project owner should lay out the requirements and desired outcome for the upcoming sprint. Once the outcomes are clear, the team collaborates to identify key ideas and tasks that should be prioritized in the next sprint. The team then breaks down each idea into a measurable work product, identifies timelines and potential roadblocks, and emerges from the meeting with a clear work plan for the next two weeks.

These planning meetings increase transparency, as everyone involved in the project gets to participate in planning new ideas and tasks. Planning meetings not only create opportunities for real time adjustments but they allow the individual team members with the best knowledge of the problem space to contribute to the solution.

## EXECUTING TASKS

The tasks assigned during Sprint Planning should be broken down into small, discrete units (called User Stories). User Stories should always be given a time estimate, and any new story should take less than one day to complete. If a story might take longer than a day, we recommend breaking the task down into smaller units.

Each User Story has two key features:

1. A clear statement of how the task directly serves a customer/donor or ties to an organizational objective (e.g. "As a Donor, I want to see my full giving history when I log into the website.")

2. A clear time estimate and ownership

Many organizations find it useful to write each story on a yellow sticky note and post it on a wall in the meeting room. The sticky notes allow you to physically arrange the work on the wall and reprioritize tasks by moving the sticky notes around. When you have enough notes on the wall to fill up your team's time, then the sprint is full. If your team is remote, tools like Trello or Asana can simulate the "sticky note" experience.

Each story in a sprint should be directly tied to the specific, key measurable organizational goal. If you can't clearly articulate how the story impacts your cause directly, you should carefully evaluate if the story is worth doing.

Again, the "end user" of the campaign, initiative, program, etc. is a vital part of tying outcomes to Sprint Planning. If you invite the stakeholders you serve into these meetings, you'll dramatically reduce the risk of working on an idea that doesn't add value. By using cross-functional teams where everyone feels ownership, you'll improve buy-in and generate better ideas.

## SETTING CONSTRAINTS

While a free flow of creative ideas during Sprint Planning is important, it can be incredibly useful to clearly define the constraints and scope of the problem you're trying to solve. Guardrails can help the team stay focused and, in the end, create better ideas. Focusing the team on a particular goal (e.g. "Increase donor retention by 10% before March 31st") is the best place to start. It can also be helpful to clearly define the tools available to accomplish the goal. ("We are allowed to change the website, email creative/copy, and social media activity. We will table other ideas and then share them with the relevant team.")

The idea of using constraints to drive improved innovation isn't new. Researchers at Harvard have produced several important insights about the power of constraints to focus teams and drive innovation. Following a 2019 study, one Harvard team summarized their findings this way:

"We reviewed 145 empirical studies on the effects of constraints on creativity and innovation, and found that individuals, teams, and organizations alike benefit from a healthy dose of constraints. It is only when the constraints become too high that they stifle creativity and innovation."[2]

In other words, appropriate constraints create a box for the team to focus on while allowing them to reach out of the box to solve problems creatively. As counterintuitive as it may feel, clear constraints are often the breeding ground for disruptive innovation.

## A QUICK TIP ON GETTING STARTED WITH AGILE: PROVING RESULTS WITH A SMALL TEAM

Moving to the Agile methodology can be a shock for many nonprofits that have relied on more traditional models for planning work. Rather than pushing your entire organization to adopt Agile, we recommend starting with a single project or team. Your initial team can help decrease the risk of Agile at your organization — and the results they produce will be a clear proof point to the rest of the organization.

I've personally worked with several nonprofits who were incredibly reluctant to adopt Agile. The increased collaboration, transparency, and willingness to change accompanying this transition felt like a

---

2   Oguz A. Acar, Murat Tarakci, and Daan van Knippenberg, "Why Constraints Are Good for Innovation," *Harvard Business Review*, November 22, 2019, https://hbr.org/2019/11/why-constraints-are-good-for-innovation.

bridge too far. In a few cases, I was able to convince the organization to temporarily test Agile on a single project within a single team. I recommend sticking with the Agile approach within your "test team" for six months before officially killing the idea. Every time a nonprofit ran this experiment, the new Agile team saw dramatic increases in team output, improved results, and team camaraderie.

In my experience, winning is contagious. Once one team starts creating successes, other teams will lean in to see what's different. And, you'll likely find that the rest of your organization will begin to naturally shift toward more Agile processes with far less pushback.

## LEARN FROM RETROSPECTIVES

As mentioned earlier, a core component of the Sprint Planning process is the ability to learn and adjust in real time. When each sprint ends, it's crucial that your team doesn't just move on to the next sprint without taking time to reflect and look at data. In most cases, the retrospective at the end of each sprint is just as important as the Sprint Planning process itself. The retrospective process allows your team to evaluate what went right and what went wrong, and what learnings can be applied to the next sprint.

In the words of Dan Heath in his groundbreaking book *Upstream*, "The postmortem for a problem can be the preamble to a solution."

Mark Miller has been consistently using retrospectives to help nonprofit clients at Historic drive outsized value. Much of Mark's retrospective work has been dramatically influenced by the book *Formula X,* which zeroes in on the retrospective practices of a Formula One racing team — and applies the process of fast-paced racing teams to businesses.

Formula One teams have one to two weeks between races to make a thousand changes and updates to the car and get it ready to compete again. They don't have time to waste, so they work quickly. Key challenges are evaluated, solutions are crafted, and tasks are assigned to different team members who lead the charge of completing each task before the next race day.

Miller describes it this way: "It's amazing how fast Formula One teams operate and how fast they make changes. They'll make up to a thousand changes to a car between races, which could be one to two weeks. And you think about how fast a nonprofit can change, to respond to something, and it's not nearly that quick. So we try to teach our clients how to embrace a different way of working because that thing that they're trying to do is really, really important to humanity, generally speaking, right?"

So what's the secret to Formula One race teams? Miller says:

"The unique advantage of Formula One teams is their use of retros. How many nonprofits do you know do weekly retros to learn and adjust? Unfortunately, that just doesn't happen. In Formula One, the race is 90 minutes, and they still do a three-to-five-hour retro on the race to improve for next time. After the race, everyone is released to go do what they're supposed to do. No one tells them what to do along the way. They just do it because they are empowered to do it. They don't have time to wait to get approval. They can't wait for permission to get the right tool or use the race simulator. They just go."

"It's the same in nonprofits. The world is changing fast and nonprofits need to use historical data to learn quickly and then empower their teams to act. For example, a few years ago, marketing automation was the big change in nonprofit technology. At this point, automation is just assumed, and AI is the newest advancement with the opportunity to change everything. That's how fast things are changing. If nonprofits want to stay relevant, raise more money, and grow their impact, they will have to learn quickly from historical data, adapt to change, and take advantage of the opportunities. And sometimes those opportunities look very, very different from traditional models."

As Miller points out, a Formula One retrospective includes the team reviewing what went well, the areas that need improvement, and what they will focus on over the next two weeks. And these retrospectives are filled with candid, data-driven feedback from every member of the racing team. Following the retrospective, every team member jumps into action. There is no political posturing or bureaucratic hoops to jump through. Each team is empowered to complete their tasks without having to wait for approval or follow a tedious process.

In the same way, nonprofit teams have the opportunity to use sprint and project retrospectives to drive accelerated learning and improved results. Following each retrospective, key learnings should be documented and then team members should be empowered to act based on insights from the previous sprint.

## SUMMARY

The Agile methodology can be the key to unlocking adaptability and innovation within your nonprofit. Versions of the Agile framework have been applied at for-profit companies for years, revolutionizing the way these organizations plan, evolve, and respond to their shifting environments. And, in the evolving world of nonprofits, it's a crucial tool to break away from the status quo by learning and responding quickly.

In most cases, it isn't realistic to migrate your entire organization to Agile at the same time. The best place to start is often the Marketing and Communications team. Marketing projects often lend themselves well to constant testing and innovation. Once you see provable results in Marketing, it will be easier to begin migrating Agile to other internal project-based teams.

# HUMAN-CENTERED DESIGN

*"It's not 'us versus them' or even 'us on behalf of them.' For a*
*design thinker it has to be 'us with them'" – Tim Brown*

In 2009, water expert and engineer Gary White and actor Matt Damon came together to create Water.org based on their shared passion to address the global water crisis. The focus of their new initiative was a new type of funding model that they called WaterCredit. While Gary's traditional "well building" projects had been successful in the past, it became clear that simply building more access points to clean water was not enough to truly solve the problem. The team at Water.org realized that there were larger systemic issues and market failures related to water access, sanitation, and local empowerment that needed to be addressed. In short, the team understood that it was time to innovate.

Today, Water.org's mission isn't simply to "build as many wells as possible." Instead, they are driven to "pioneer market-driven financial solutions to the global water crisis." On the surface, this statement may seem like marketing fluff. But, those who have spent time with Water.org know that they take the "pioneering" aspect of their work very seriously.

And it shows. According to Water.org, the organization has mobilized more than $4.6 billion in capital supporting water safety projects in 11 countries affecting over 58 million people.

To create this impact, Water.org shifted its strategy from simply building wells to creating innovative solutions that would increase access to safe and sanitary drinking water. One of the most impactful initiatives generated by Water.org's "WaterCredit" approach was the creation of WaterEquity (waterequity.com), an asset management fund that invests in opportunities in the water and sanitation sector. Specifically, the fund facilitates large capital investments in enterprises, infrastructure, and financial institutions to mobilize systemic changes related to clean water.

WaterEquity was an important step in building a solution for the supply of capital for water and sanitation loans. However, that project was just the beginning and ultimately spawned several additional innovative initiatives within Water.org.

Josh Gunkel spent almost five years at Water.org as the Director of Technology, Impact, and Innovation. During his tenure, Josh had a front-row seat to the creation of WaterEquity and the rest of the portfolio of solutions all designed to accelerate impact and enable as many families as possible to meet their water and sanitation needs.

As he describes it, Water.org was already seeing good fundraising success with traditional strategies and donor programs, but they were committed to pursuing a new solution that would deploy large amounts of capital quickly against one of the world's toughest problems.

As the WaterEquity program expanded, the Water.org team realized that "everyday donors" weren't able to fully participate in this new innovative project. At its heart, WaterEquity was designed as a fund for large investors, but smaller donors had no way to give to these important systemic changes. Opening the door to more traditional donors to invest in their new capital deployment strategy would require a more innovative approach.

"To explore bridging the gap with smaller donors we worked with the fabulous folks at IDEO. We started from the beginning and did the human-centered design work to understand the real need and insights in the space we were exploring. We took the time to talk with our constituents, ask probing questions, and truly understand the desires of our potential donor base. We landed on this amazing intersection of people having what we called 'lazy money.' Effectively, our potential donors had unused capacity for generosity. They wanted to do more good, but they perceived that good wouldn't be accomplished through traditional donations."

What came out of the sessions with IDEO and constituent interviews was the idea for a consumer-facing app that would let more traditional donors participate in WaterEquity by putting their money directly into an "impact account." Water.org would then bucket the donations together across the donor network to create larger capital investments in the WaterEquity model.

They called their new mobile app Float (get it?!).

Through the app, users could "bank" their money in their accounts and help fund the microfinance loans being used by families to meet their water and sanitation needs.

The Float project was the direct result of interviewing constituents to identify a set of deeper desires and opportunities. Rather than assuming that traditional fundraising methods would solve the problem, Water.org spent time talking with potential donors, stakeholders, and unaffiliated people on the street to understand their underlying motivations and desire for impact. That journey of empathy became the seed for innovation.

During our chat, Josh was quick to point out that the Float project was a casualty of COVID-19. The concept was temporarily put on ice as Water.org weathered the COVID storm (though we're all hopeful that the idea will be resurrected in the future.) As with any project, not everything in Water.org's quest to address the needs around water and sanitation has gone according to plan. But rather than slowing down based on the inevitable stumbles along the way, Water.org has focused on listening to its constituents, learning quickly, and changing its approach based on the feedback they receive. Instead of spending years in planning and speculation, the team at Water.org cast a big vision based on authentic feedback from their community and then began shifting organizational priorities to hit their goal. The entire team embraces the question "What do our stakeholders want and need?" to learn and adapt quickly toward a more innovative solution.

## THE TRADITIONAL TOP-DOWN APPROACH TO NEW IDEAS

The story of Water.org is encouraging because it demonstrates the power of rapid change based on real constituent feedback. The team at Water.org saw changing needs in the world, recognized an opportunity, and adapted quickly to rise to the occasion. But, unlike Water.org, the impetus for change at many nonprofits doesn't originate from the constituents that are most impacted by the cause. The truth is that most nonprofits rely on a top-down approach to innovation that is often directed by leaders in the organization who are disconnected from the real-world problem.

Many nonprofits rely on hierarchical structures, with a board of directors or leadership team at the top that makes strategic decisions for the organization — and team members who simply work to implement the board-approved plan throughout the year. And, in many cases, the leaders who recommend new ideas often have very little personal interaction with the actual communities connected to the work of the cause. Many of these ideas can be well-intentioned, but they lack meaningful feedback from constituents and, as a result, fail to have a significant impact.

## THE IMPORTANCE OF HUMAN-CENTERED DESIGN

Fortunately, there's a more effective "bottoms-up" approach to driving innovation that puts your donors and community at the center of your innovation journey. Rather than relying on leaders within the organization to fix problems in a vacuum, human-centered design flips the script by working directly with constituents to determine which solutions will be most effective.

Human-centered design helps organizations co-create solutions shoulder-to-shoulder with their community by asking questions to unearth the community's true needs and desires. And, importantly, it helps nonprofit leaders see past the obvious symptoms of the problem and instead focus on upstream systemic solutions.

The concept of human-centered design (HCD) was first described by Stanford professor John Arnold in the 1950s as a means to improve product design by starting from a human-first perspective. HCD has since been refined by the Stanford Design School and countless product development companies around the world. Companies like IDEO, who helped drive innovation at Water.org, now lead with human-centered design as their primary driver of sustainable innovation.

At its heart, HCD is an iterative approach to problem-solving that centers around the specific needs of a community. It places people at the forefront of the process and relies on the perspectives and experiences of end users to drive the development of new ideas.

For nonprofits, human-centered design represents a more empathetic approach to fundraising and program design. Rather than creating solutions in a vacuum, nonprofits who leverage HCD start by listening closely to the needs of their donors and community. They move beyond the basic functional requirements of a campaign or service, and seek to understand the emotional and psychological needs of the people they serve. HCD-driven nonprofits aim to create solutions that are intuitive, emotionally resonant, and aligned with the real-life needs of the community.

Central to HCD is the continuous feedback loop between your constituents, community, and team. At every stage of development, nonprofits who leverage HCD work to ensure that their fundraising, marketing, and program initiatives align closely with the expectations and desires of the people they serve.

The importance of human-centered design cannot be overstated in today's rapidly evolving world. It has become a cornerstone of successful innovation for many leading nonprofits. By placing your constituents at the center of the innovation process, HCD helps ensure that your work will be fully embraced once it's launched.

Design thinking also helps reduce the risk of costly bad assumptions and design flaws that are often unnoticed when a new project is launched. From the earliest stages of development, HCD helps ensure that your program and fundraising initiatives address real-world problems rather than hypothetical ones. This people-first approach fosters a culture of empathy and collaboration among your team, community, and constituents — ultimately resulting in campaigns and services that have a meaningful impact on people's lives.

Mark Miller at Historic Agency relies on the human-centered approach as he drives innovation for his nonprofit clients.

"Nonprofits struggle to put their audience first," Miller says. "But how do you have empathy for all the different stakeholders that you have to engage with? Not just the donor or the community you're serving. Nonprofits will be really passionate about global missions, or the environment, or the unhoused — but they tend to fail to have empathy for other stakeholders, such as the communities they serve, their volunteers, or their donors. Empathy and design thinking will help you become more effective in serving those audiences, creating deeper engagement, spreading out and affecting revenue, opportunities, and impact."

"Technological and cultural changes are putting tremendous pressure on nonprofits. At the same time, the private sector is using social impact as a form of business marketing. These shifts are creating a growing distance between nonprofits and the constituents they serve. The only hope that nonprofits have to grow through these changes is design thinking and adaptive organizational design. You have to be rooted in a clear 'why' that ties back to the needs of the people you serve."

For Miller, human-centered design can also profoundly impact your team, culture, and brand.

"A lot of times, we'll deploy systems and processes to nonprofits, but the process doesn't work because, at some level, it is antithetical to the values of your brand and the community that you serve. These misaligned systems weaken the team's ability to act in a way that's on-brand and serves the organization's values and community. And so, at every touchpoint, your team needs to ask, are these systems human-centered? Do they align with our principles and values? How do the people in the organization experience these processes? Because the answers to those questions will bleed out into how your people interact with your donors, volunteers, etc."

## GETTING STARTED WITH HUMAN-CENTERED DESIGN

There is a never-ending supply of helpful content on human-centered design from the Stanford Design School, IDEO, and others. But to help start your journey, I've provided the basic framework from Stanford for moving toward a more human-centered approach at your nonprofit. This process can be modified to fit your organization's needs, though the overarching framework provides a clear roadmap for driving innovative outcomes in a more structured way.

The key to success with any new HCD initiative is to lead with donor and community empathy. The most effective nonprofits use the following standard HCD steps to shorten the distance between their team and the needs of the people they serve.

### 1. Empathize

The first step in human-centered design is all about listening and empathy. This step starts with research, surveys, and probing questions — all of which come from a place of open and honest curiosity. Do your best to avoid any assumptions about what your community needs. Keep an open mind. And, above all, be guided by the underlying needs and desires of the people you serve.

This will mean getting as close to your end audience as possible. If you work in Program, try to spend time with your community and experience your program services firsthand. Survey your program constituents and ask open-ended questions to help identify hidden influences you may be missing. If you're in Fundraising, spend time in authentic conversations with donors. Then, "secret shop" your fundraising experience by giving to your organization. Put yourself in the shoes of your constituents. How would they feel? What do they need? What are their pain points?

One of my favorite methods to get to the root of any problem is to ask "why" five times. Sometimes referred to as the 5Y approach, this technique was developed by Toyota founder Sakichi Toyoda to better identify underlying issues within a system. Instead of assuming someone's first answer to a question is complete, the 5Y approach mandates that you continue asking "why" after every answer to get to the root issue. This approach may feel silly at times. In fact, it often reminds me of my nine-year-old daughter peppering me with "why" questions from the back of our car! But continuing to ask the question "why" even after it feels uncomfortable can be an invaluable tool for moving past surface-level responses and digging deeper into upstream problems and underlying motivations.

## 2. Define

After you've spent time listening and empathizing, it's time to define the problem that you want to solve. Dig deep into all the notes that you took during the empathize phase. Try not to approach the definition process with any foregone conclusions or presuppositions. Do your best to define the problem BEHIND the problem, and understand the root cause. You should exit this stage with a clear point of view about a specific challenge or opportunity within your community.

It's also important to note that this process works best when you are focused on solving a related set of problems within the community. You may uncover a myriad of pain points during the empathize phase, but it's important to stay focused. So, during the define phase, pick a related set of problems that continuously emerge within your community. Look for commonalities and repeated phrasing to help you hone in on the best problem to tackle first.

If you're unsure about how well you've defined your problem, play it back to your community to ensure it resonates with them. Ask for additional insights into areas that you may have overlooked.

### 3. Ideate

Once your problem is clearly defined, you can begin generating ideas that address a real problem experienced by the people you serve. Rather than focusing on a single idea to fix the problem you've defined, work with your team to generate dozens of ideas. Don't be afraid to suggest audacious changes. Work to break through any fixed mindsets that may have limited your thinking in the past. You'll have the opportunity to refine your ideas later in the process.

### 4. Prototype

During the prototyping step, you'll refine and combine your ideas to zero in on a smaller number of potential solutions. The goal is to determine which ideas 1) best meet the community's needs, 2) are most feasible based on the team and budget constraints, and 3) are sustainable over the long haul.

For each idea, it's crucial to determine the "Minimum Viable Product" (MVP) you'll need to validate the idea with your community. As you may recall from the Agile methodology, an MVP is essentially a low-cost prototype that allows your team to show your work to a small number of people in the community and get validation or feedback. MVPs are critically important in both fundraising and program work. You should constantly ask, "What is the minimum effort required to prove that this idea works in the real world?"

On your Program team, this often means piloting the idea with a small subset of your community to get feedback. In Fundraising, creating an MVP will often involve segmenting out a small portion of your donor database to test the new idea or message. This process might include initiatives like 1) buying social media ads to test a new message, 2) split testing an email with a small segment of donors, 3) hosting a small event to gauge donor interest in a concept, etc. Based on the feedback you receive in prototyping, you can try another prototype or iterate on the original concept until it meets the needs of your community. The key is to stay collaborative and constantly solicit feedback from the people you serve.

## 5. Test

After you have a viable prototype, it's time to scale and test your new solution. Make sure to maintain a sense of empathy and collaboration throughout the implementation and testing process. Change is hard, but it's infinitely easier when you have strong support from your community. Bring other teams along for the ride by sharing learnings from your previous steps. And, when possible, give your donors or community visibility into your process. Remember, transparency is the name of the game with human-centered design.

To effectively test the idea, create measurable milestones along the way that tie to KPIs. Continuously look at the impact and engagement related to the new solution. Commit your team to iterating on the solution in order to make it incrementally better over time. And, importantly, once the new idea is launched, continue to listen for feedback to ensure your solution is meeting the real needs of actual people. Stay open-minded and maintain a willingness to change and adapt.

## A DEEPER LOOK AT LOOK AT EMPATHY

The steps outlined above may seem straightforward in theory. In fact, you may already be implementing some version of this process within your organization today, but you're still not seeing results. You're polling your communities, you're asking them what you should do better, and you're getting a lot of the same repetitive feedback that echoes the things you already know. While you're trying your best to listen to your constituents, the first step of "Empathize" never seems to drive valuable fodder for innovation.

There's a popular quote attributed to Henry Ford that perfectly summarizes this issue. When asked if he received customer feedback before designing the car, Ford purportedly said, "If I had asked people what they wanted, they would have said faster horses."

Whether or not Ford ever actually uttered these words is debatable. But the truth still applies. Most of your constituents simply aren't capable of imagining a world that doesn't exist. Like you, they will likely default to the simplest answers or tried and true solutions, without ever fully reimagining what could be.

With that in mind, our job is never to simply ask our constituents, "What do you want?" Our job is to unearth the underlying set of problems that are preventing them from living their best lives, and then reimagine creative solutions to those problems. In other words, we need to move beyond simply interviewing constituents, and instead do the harder work of "empathy gathering."

Jacob Hancock is the Executive Director at Seeds, an innovation lab for nonprofits. He's also an adjunct professor at Rollins College where he teaches human-centered design practices within the business school. Jacob believes that "there's a thorough misunderstanding of what empathy gathering is, and it's because we're not trained to do it well. A lot of people think that simply conducting surveys will help them arrive at the solution to a particular problem, but they aren't asking the right questions."

Hancock's favorite story to share about empathy gathering is the check-in process at the Orlando airport. He starts the story by describing a fictitious airport staff member who has been tasked with reimagining the airport check-in experience. Naturally, this eager new leader might start by asking flyers a series of survey questions like, "What's the most difficult part of your check-in experience at the Orlando International Airport?"

Hancock goes on to explain, "What do you think is the most common response you'll get to that question? It's security, right? Everyone is going to say the exact same answer every single time if you catch them off-guard with that question. Security. Everyone's going to respond the exact same way. These days, most people have already checked into their flight on their phones, they carry their bags on instead of checking, so their only real obstacle to getting to their gate is going through security. So when you ask your survey question, you prompt a simple response that confirms what you already know."

But if you try a totally different approach, using what Hancock refers to as "empathy prompts," you could get travelers to tell you a completely new story.

Let's say this staff member asks this instead: "Tell me about the last time you arrived at the Orlando International Airport to depart. Describe the process and how it felt."

Now, suddenly, if I'm the traveler, I'm not thinking about the security line. Instead, my response might go something like this...

*I pulled up to the airport, got out of my car, got my bag, and I was about to go inside. But then my four children who are in the back of my car started calling, "Daddy, you're going to be gone for 10 days, so you gotta say bye to us." So I got back into the car and started hugging and kissing each of my four children. All the while, the traffic official in the orange vest was running around us, blowing his whistle and yelling at me, "You can't sit here! You got to go! You got to go!" My stress level was through the roof. But quite frankly, I was thinking to myself, "Screw you, dude. I'm saying bye to my kids." Then, after I said goodbye, I went inside and went through security.*

When you hear this story, you quickly understand the traveler's biggest issue wasn't the security process, but rather the high-stress drop-off zone outside the airport. You get a totally new perspective and a real user story that clearly details a very human experience. Now, instead of going back to the drawing board for the hundredth time trying to figure out how to make TSA more efficient, you have a new perspective on the check-in process you can address to help make your traveler's experience better.

But most organizations aren't asking these kinds of questions. Many organizations make the mistake of thinking they know what their community is going to say, and they ask survey questions that confirm their assumptions.

"It's just confirmation bias," Hancock says. "We do that all the time. Instead, let's ask the question as if we have no clue what their answer is going to be. We take on a real learner mindset and we listen to understand, not to agree. To do this, you have to provide empathy prompts. 'Tell me about a time when…' Then you listen to their story and extrapolate the person's real problem, rather than fitting them into a trend."

"For many of us in the faith-based nonprofit world, we've been involved in ministry for so long that we're convinced we know our end users so well that we can anticipate how they're going to answer these questions. And you're wrong. You can't. You don't gain true empathy and when it's time to reframe and innovate, your assumptions are already wrong. So when you're attempting to come up with something that would be disruptive or radical, it generally fails to come together because you didn't truly gain empathy, or you didn't spend enough time and think creatively in ideation. The problem might be that you have enough ideas. You've just filtered out the best ideas by making bad assumptions."

Humans are unpredictable. You could be married to someone for 50 years and still be surprised by their thoughts, feelings, and experiences. HCD allows you to look beyond the surface, beyond the preconceived notions and ideas you have about whom you're serving, and actually take the time to get to know the people behind the work.

---

# CASE STUDY
## JEREMY VALLERAND AND ATLAS FREE

Jeremy Vallerand is the President and CEO of Atlas Free, a nonprofit organization dedicated to eradicating sexual exploitation and sex trafficking. At Atlas, human-centered design practices are integrated into the strategic planning process to respond to the most urgent opportunities based on shifting trends in the communities in which they're working.

Atlas has created a unique strategic process that enables the team to evaluate trends in the culture, the economy, and the fight against human trafficking — and then quickly re-orient their operations to respond to shifts in real time. Instead of remaining static as the world changes, the Atlas framework allows them to respond to the shifting needs of their community, and position themselves in the best possible place to create impact.

"One of the tools we use comes from a group called the Patterson Center, and it's called the StratOp Process," Vallerand explains. "It's a strategic planning framework that we use that pulls people from all departments and brings them together to create our annual plan. But the key part of this process is that we start by evaluating the macro trends that are out there. What's happening in the culture, in the economy, in the fight against human trafficking, in the nonprofit sector broadly? We listen to our teams and experts on the ground — and then make sure everyone is bringing their unique perspective to the table. All these trends come together and it's up to us to spot the opportunities."

In other words, the Atlas team starts with listening and empathy. They include team members from all levels of the organization in the strategic process, and then intentionally pull in feedback from partners, cultural trends, and the communities they are serving.

"Now, I'm wired as an entrepreneur," he admits. "I'm attracted to the shiny opportunities. So we have an exercise where we go through every potential opportunity on a regular cadence and map it on an opportunity matrix that asks, 'What is the opportunity and what is its potential risk to the organization?' The opportunity could be quantified in terms of programmatic impact, lives impacted or saved, or it could be from a fundraising standpoint of revenue generated or donors engaged. So opportunity is relative to the sector of the organization."

"Risk is evaluated the same way. What's the financial risk? The organizational risk? Obviously, human trafficking can be a contentious issue, and it intersects with a lot of hot-button issues. So we say, 'We think we could advocate for this, but here are the groups that are going to come after us if we do that.' Or, 'Here's the revenue, we can make this impact.' So every opportunity we encounter has to run through this exercise and be touched by our cross-functional team."

Using this matrix, Vallerand's team can make strategic decisions quickly without getting bogged down with rigid structures. They talk openly about the risk and impact of each opportunity on their community to reach clarity around the best ideas. They are also diligent in soliciting feedback from their community along the way. As a result, this process allows the Atlas team to dive headfirst into each new opportunity with increased conviction and team alignment.

"At the end of the process, we're looking at the opportunity level vs. the risk level. By and large, we try to stick to things that fall into what we call the 'gold mine' where there's high opportunity and minimized risk based on what we've learned from our team and community. Again, we're okay with risk if we can mitigate it. But we need to have buy-in from the entire departmental team."

The discipline of efficiently evaluating risk vs reward allows Atlas to stay agile without putting the larger organization at risk. Their strategic process allows them to analyze opportunities on the ground and decide whether or not they will create a meaningful impact on the organization's larger mission. The strategy also helps the team remain human-centered, involving all stakeholders in the decision-making process.

For Vallerand, this process starts with creating a human-centered organization where every team member and donor has a seat at the table.

"We believe every human being was created with inherent dignity and equal value. So that has to apply universally across the organization. We don't look at our donors and just see their money. They're a person, created with equal value, and they're looking for a connection and to make an impact. Our job is to invite them into the journey."

"And at the end of the day, we create this beautiful equation that incorporates every piece. There are human beings expressing a desire to live in a world where there is hope, where lives can be changed, and where impact can be made. Everybody wants that. Everybody wants to know that, at the end of the day, they have the agency to participate in improving the world around them."

## SUMMARY

At the end of the day, nonprofits exist for people. The people who benefit from the work and the people who make the work possible. Nonprofits must stay tightly connected with the communities they serve to maximize their impact and drive innovation. Human-centered design provides a clear framework for creating empathy with the people on the frontlines of your cause. At its core, HCD empowers organizations to work shoulder-to-shoulder with their community to drive innovation and maximize impact.

Organizations that start with their constituents and work backward find solutions faster. They avoid wasting time and resources on projects that don't address real needs. At the heart of every nonprofit is a community of humans. Start there, and the rest will follow.

# MANAGING CHANGE

*"In times of change, learners inherit the earth, while the learned find themselves beautifully equipped to deal with a world that no longer exists." – Eric Hoffer*

I hate to state the obvious...but innovation requires change, and change is hard.

In our work at Virtuous, we have a front-row seat to transformational change and innovation within nonprofit teams. If a nonprofit changes its donor management software or undergoes other types of digital transformation, there will undoubtedly be pain. After all, change is hard. But it's also unavoidable. And organizations that are able to not just "manage" transformational change but use change as a springboard to new opportunities will emerge as the true innovation leaders in the nonprofit sector.

When the team at Operation Mobilization (OM) decided to remove their legacy CRM system and move onto our CRM platform (Virtuous), they only had six months remaining in their existing CRM contract. The OM team was standing on a burning platform, and a successful transition would require rapid cultural and process changes across the organization. The leadership team at OM knew they wouldn't have the time to slowly bring the team along over the course of a couple of years. They needed immediate and unwavering buy-in from their team to quickly learn, adapt, and embrace change.

In one of the boldest and most creative moves I've seen in my 25 years in enterprise technology, the CTO at OM had everyone on their team sign an internal "contract" that pledged their commitment to embrace the change. While the contract was somewhat tongue-in-cheek, it helped ensure everyone at OM understood that 1) things were changing, 2) some stuff would be hard, 3) we're all in this together, and 4) we have each other's backs.

The idea of an internal contract to help facilitate change might seem silly, but I've rarely seen a team so committed to successfully adapting to change. Over the next six months, everyone I talked to at OM seemed willing to learn and evolve to serve their constituents and teammates better. The contract served as a tangible symbol of the organization's commitment to change, and it provided a reminder to team members on days when the going got tough that they were all in it together.

If "internal contracts" aren't your style, you may appreciate the more lighthearted approach to change created by the University of Central Missouri (UCM).

Like OM, UCM was transitioning to our CRM software and wanted to ensure their team was fully equipped for success. In addition to typical change-management best practices, UCM decided to inject a healthy dose of fun into their team training and enablement. Rather than relying solely on traditional training on the new platform, they gamified the training program and created a CRM-specific version of Jeopardy! for their team members. Just in case you missed that... UCM created a full-scale version of Donor Software Jeopardy! Not only did the gamification of their CRM transition make training fun, but it increased learning and accelerated buy-in across the organization. It also generated excitement about the process and turned what might have felt like an overwhelming change into a team-building experience.

## CHEESE MOVING IN CHARITIES

My favorite book on change management is the business classic *Who Moved My Cheese?* There are certainly more sophisticated and academic books available on this topic, but few management books pack so much punch in so few pages.

At its core, responding to change is a people and mindset problem, not just a process problem. In *Who Moved My Cheese?*, author Spencer Johnson sums up the mindset problem associated with change this way: "What you are afraid of is never as bad as what you imagine. The fear you let build up in your mind is worse than the situation that actually exists."

Managing change is about managing fear — your own fear and the collective fear of your organization. And, in some ways, it's about cultivating a healthy fear of the alternative to change: dying a slow death at the altar of the "status quo."

Unfortunately, some segments of the nonprofit sector have become synonymous with "institutional inertia." In other words, change has been made almost impossible by the bureaucratic weight of the organization. Waiting for changes at a large nonprofit can sometimes feel like watching a glacier move. As the outside world accelerates, many nonprofits creep along, making small incremental changes, painfully gaining ground inch by inch.

In many traditional nonprofits, leaders are consistently confronted with team members who are afraid to have their "cheese moved." They relentlessly push back on innovation with statements like, "We've never done it that way before," "That will never work," and "Our donors aren't on that social media platform." They are anchored to the fear of the unknown — unable and unwilling to learn and grow for the sake of the cause.

The good news is that it doesn't have to be this way. Change is unavoidable, and everyone's cheese will move eventually. But, the best nonprofits embrace change and develop an organizational growth mindset. Using the right processes, culture, and incentives, great nonprofit leaders bring the entire organization together to embrace change with open collaboration and genuine excitement. Instead of dragging the team along kicking and screaming, good change management leaders position change, not as something being done <u>to</u> the team, but as a journey the team takes together.

As with human-centered design, change management starts with the people closest to your cause. While it's important to understand your goals and the problems you're facing, you won't make real progress without understanding the people whose lives will be most impacted, both positively and negatively, by the change. Leaders who implement change successfully start with their team members and figure out the mindset adjustments needed to achieve organizational buy-in. That is the only way change works.

## WHAT MAKES CHANGE SO HARD FOR NONPROFITS?

Nonprofits are filled with amazing people who desperately want to create a positive impact. Creating CHANGE in the world is literally the reason we all started working in the nonprofit space to begin with. So, if driving change is at the heart of every nonprofit, why does change within our walls seem so hard?

In 1994, Harvard researchers attempted to answer this question by looking at positive and negative outcomes from organizations that navigated large changes. The study revealed four core drivers (or killers) of change within the organizations in the study.[3] *Failing to acknowledge any of these four drivers will inevitably lead to bottlenecks in implementing change.*

1. DURATION – Work cycles with short duration and consistent inspection and accountability (see the Agile practice!)

   *Are you reviewing progress every two weeks? Do you have clear, measurable milestones along the way? Are you reviewing risks and learnings with your team as you go?*

2. INTEGRITY – Cohesive, qualified, capable teams

   *Do you have a consistent team working on the project? Are they qualified to do the job required? Is there strong leadership for the team?*

3. COMMITMENT – Strong buy-in from staff AND leadership

---

3    Harold L. Sirkin, Perry Keenan, and Alan Jackson, "The Hard Side of Change Management," Harvard Business Review (October 2005): https://hbr.org/2005/10/the-hard-side-of-change-management.

*Do you have clear executive sponsorship? Did you spell out the "why" of the change to your team and create full buy-in?*

4. EFFORT – How much additional work is required from staff beyond their normal job

*Are you asking your team to put in far more hours than their typical job? Is the effort required realistic, or do other projects need to be deprioritized?*

These four principles (often referred to as DICE) have been successfully used by countless organizations over the past 30 years to diagnose and fix blockers to change. If any of these four principles are lacking in a project, the risk of failure increases substantially. We recommend using this simple framework at the beginning of any innovative project or significant change at your organization to quickly calibrate the organization for success.

Larger organizations can even use a "DICE Score" to rate the risks associated with a large systemic change. While this book isn't a great place to provide a detailed explanation of DICE Scoring, if you're facing a large systemic change at your organization, it would be worth a deeper dive into this topic.

## THE COMMON PITFALLS FOR CHANGE AT NONPROFITS, WITH MAUREEN WALBEOFF

The DICE Framework provides clear principles for successfully accelerating change, but several common pitfalls within nonprofit teams prevent the elements of DICE from being fully realized.

We sat down with Maureen Wallbeoff to chat about some of the common blockers of change in the nonprofit sector. Maureen is a leading nonprofit consultant and technology coach who has spent the past 15 years helping nonprofit teams innovate and drive change.

Unsurprisingly, our conversation addressed several aspects of the DICE framework including Commitment, Effort, and Integrity. Wallbeoff was quick to point out that many nonprofit professionals are hesitant about change because they've failed attempts at change so many times in the past. "I think that makes people flinchy," says Wallbeoff. "Here comes another change. We didn't achieve success the last time. I'm in a self-protective mode right from the jump."

Getting the necessary Commitment from the team can be incredibly difficult when previous attempts at change have been mismanaged or the Effort required from the staff was too high. "If too much is changing or the process feels chaotic to the team, they're going to put up some resistance, because we all have a finite tolerance for how much change we can handle successfully at one time," says Wallbeoff.

Wallbeoff was also quick to recognize that successful change management at nonprofits starts with strong collaboration. "Collaborative work is the secret. You have to bring people from these different teams together and encourage them to work together so that there are no surprises. People have each other's backs. Everybody's looped in on what's happening. And it's much easier to celebrate successes or to do a debrief on learnings if everybody's at the table from the beginning. You can't just say, 'This is the Fundraising team's project,' or "This is the Marketing and Communication team's job.' That's a problem." Similar to the DICE framework, Wallbeoff's work with nonprofits has consistently demonstrated that the Integrity of cohesive and collaborative teams is essential for meaningful change.

In her work with Fundraising teams specifically, Wallbeoff has also found that nonprofits often lack the fundamental data and infrastructure to measure and support change.

"Nonprofits don't have time to creatively innovate and test things with their supporters because they're bringing some fundamental data hygiene and data metrics issues with them, and that tends to make change hard," Wallbeoff says.

"I've got a wonderful organization that I work with that has great tools, smart people who work well together, and just checks all the boxes for a high-functioning team. But they don't know whether a donor is a new donor or not. So they have pushed pause on setting up a new donor welcome series because they're afraid they're going to welcome someone who has actually been giving for a long time. Rather than tackling their database issues, they do nothing. Their energy is spent with talk of, 'Ooh, I wish we could,' but they just feel stuck before they even start, because they need to clean up their data. And dealing with data hygiene issues isn't the fun part about innovation. I think that that tends to put a bit of a damper on people's enthusiasm. They come up with an idea, people get excited about it, they start to plan it out, and then they hit a roadblock — that has been a known roadblock for a long time — and they just stop."

For Wallbeoff, these issues are often exacerbated because nonprofit teams react in the moment instead of proactively planning for change. "I think most of us are very reactive, and so we don't look ahead three months, four months, five months and say, 'In May we're going to start working on X. And we're going to test some things in October. And by the time November comes around, we have enough information and technical setup to innovate.' Many nonprofits are generally 90% reactive, 10% proactive. And I'd love to see it get to 80/20. I think if 20% of the time, we made a standard practice of looking ahead and making plans, and ensuring we have the bandwidth to see those plans through to fruition, we'd all feel much more successful. Our supporter engagement campaigns and fundraising performance will see big benefits from this proactive approach. This is something our industry really needs help with. We need to figure it out."

## HOW WE COACH CHANGE MANAGEMENT AT VIRTUOUS

While much of your innovation journey will be focused on learning and testing in an insulated environment, the final step in any large-scale innovation project is systemic, organizational change. How your organization is able to manage change will largely dictate the success of the innovation.

At Virtuous, we've helped thousands of nonprofit leaders navigate transformational technology change. We've also accumulated hundreds of key learnings and experimented with multiple processes to zero in on a set of core principles that drive success.

Scott Richards has spent the last 13 years training teams and managing technology change for nonprofits. Scott currently serves as the Director of User Experience and Research at Virtuous, and he has an undying passion for helping nonprofits break free from the status quo. Rather than tell you about our change management process myself, I've recruited Scott to explain our approach here at

Virtuous and provide a few examples of how we've seen nonprofits successfully navigate change.

### *From Scott Richards:*

While team members at a nonprofit may go through multiple technology changes in their career, just say the words "CRM conversion," and you'll see them start to sweat. The weight of changing your core software can feel completely overwhelming without a clear game plan. But one of the benefits of our work at Virtuous is that we get to help organizations navigate this type of complex software change every day.

The model we use for coaching organizations through the change process is a framework that's been used by countless other organizations. In fact, you may have already seen a similar graphic to the one below during a previous change management project.

Adapted from Knoster, T (1991) Presentation in TASH Conference, Washington, D. C., Adapted by Knoster from Enterprise Group, Ltd.

The above graphic represents the Knoster model for managing complex change. The Knoster model is widely regarded as the best way to distill the needs and experience of managing change in any organization. Across the top of the diagram, you can see the five crucial elements required to successfully navigate change: Vision, Skills, Incentives, Resources, and an Action Plan. And then, in the far right column, you can see the outcome when any of the core elements is missing.

In my work managing change with hundreds of nonprofits, I've consistently seen just how accurate this model is.

The core components of the Knoster Model may seem a little "fuzzy" at first glance, so let's take a closer look at the definition and the application of each element. To add context, we'll look at how Operation Mobilization, the nonprofit mentioned at the beginning of this chapter, was able to address each of these as part of its successful transition.

## Vision

Everything starts with a Vision. Your vision for the end state of a project allows everyone on your team to understand just what things will look like once you've made a change. Successful leaders are highly skilled at "vision-casting," and the ability of your leadership to clearly articulate the new world you are moving toward will be a key driving force in successful change.

Carmine Gallo, who has written a number of books on Steve Jobs and the success of Apple, shared the importance of Jobs' vision-casting skills with *Forbes*. He tells the story of interviewing Rob Campbell, himself a tech CEO, about Campbell's first meeting with Jobs in 1977:

> *"What is your vision for the personal computer?" Campbell asked Jobs. Campbell said what happened next still gives him goose bumps. "Steve Jobs was a magical storyteller," Campbell told me. "For the next*

*hour, he talked about how personal computers were going to change the world. He painted a picture of how it would change everything about the way we worked, educated our children and entertained ourselves. You couldn't help but buy in."* **Vision**, *said Campbell, was the one thing that separated Steve Jobs from the others.*

But still, what is Vision? And why is it so important in managing change?

Put simply, creating a Vision involves painting a picture for everyone on your team of what the future holds. What will it be like once the change is successful and your new tools or processes become part of the day-to-day? If you are implementing new software, what existing systems will the new software replace? Who will use it, for what, and how often? What will you be able to do that you couldn't before? If you are innovating in other key areas of your organization, who are the key beneficiaries of the change? What pain is it solving? How will they feel when the pain is addressed?

When implementing new internal processes, be explicit in spelling out exactly what the new process will look like. How will it impact the team tasked with executing the process? Who will have new roles and responsibilities? How will it impact the broader organization? Providing a clear destination for the entire team is crucial if you want everyone to arrive together with their sanity intact.

To be clear, innovation involves stepping out into the unknown. This means it's impossible to design every detail of the desired end-state from the beginning. Great vision casting means being vulnerable enough to say "I don't know everything today, but I'm committed to learning as we go in order to achieve the best outcome."

In the case of Operation Mobilization, their leadership helped cast a vision by scheduling several internal informational sessions at the start of their implementation process, and they required every employee to attend a session. These sessions included a presentation that laid out 1) the vision for implementing and using the new software, 2) the teams that would be using the system, and 3) which software systems would be replaced or retained. They acknowledged that the change would be hard but shared a clear vision for what the ultimate future would look like on the new system. Team members were invited to ask questions or voice concerns (this is another critical element we'll focus on later), and a member of the Virtuous team was on hand to provide an overview of the platform and address any technical questions. These initial sessions were vital and allowed the entire team to understand the vision for their platform change.

Not to state the obvious, but the result of a clearly communicated vision from leadership is clarity throughout the team. And the absence of a clear vision results in team confusion and ineffectiveness.

## Skills

Taking on any new project can be massively frustrating if you don't have the skills required for the task. Just ask anyone who has taken on a DIY home improvement project for the first time. Managing change is no different.

If you want to launch a new fundraising strategy, you'll need someone with training or previous experience in that domain. If you're going to implement new software, your team will need to learn how to use it properly. If you're going to implement a new process, you'll need to train the team on how the process works (and document it for the future). If you are changing the structure of your programs, anyone taking on a new role will need to be trained to succeed in their new role.

Upleveling your team's skills should be a continuous focus at any nonprofit, but skills assessment and growth are even more critical when planning for change. The reality is that some members of your team may not be able to acquire the required skills fast enough to keep up with the change. Before moving into any significant new initiative, it's important to ask the following questions about your current team:

- Are there skill gaps that we need to hire for that are core to the success of the change?

- Are there skill gaps that we can close using consultants or an outside agency?

- Do we need to update the job descriptions and/or compensation plans of team members to better reflect the new expectations?

Building team skills should go far beyond just watching a handful of YouTube tutorials or participating in a one-time course. If you expect your team to navigate change successfully, their training should be measurable, verifiable, and intentional. And it should be a continuous process, with multiple checkpoints and assessments to ensure everyone is on track.

To start, all team learning needs to be spaced out, leaving time between each session for learners to practice what they have learned — and ideally, some time to struggle with new practices or concepts. In his book *Range: Why Generalists Triumph in a Specialized World*, David Epstein talks about the value of "desirable difficulties" in enhancing learning:

> *Desirable difficulties like testing and spacing make knowledge stick. It becomes durable. Desirable difficulties like making connections and interleaving make knowledge flexible, useful for problems that never appeared in training. All slow down learning and make performance suffer, in the short term.*

In short, you'll need to allow more time for everyone to develop the skills they need to be successful. While quick fixes may seem like efficiency gains in the short term, they can hamper the efficacy of your change in the long term.

Carolyn Dewar and Scott Keller, principals with McKinsey & Company, similarly advocate for additional time and learning reinforcement. They also point out that it's vital to factor in the thoughts and emotions of your team when mapping out a training program:

> *Consider a bank that through a benchmarking exercise discovered that its sales per banker were lagging behind those of the competition. After finding that bankers spent too little time with customers and too much time on paperwork, the bank set about reengineering the loan-origination process in order to maximize customer-facing time. Unfortunately, six*

*months later, the levels of improvement were far lower than envisioned.*

*A further investigation, with an eye to the bankers' mind-sets rather than their behaviors, revealed that they simply found customer interactions uncomfortable and therefore preferred paperwork. This feeling was driven by a combination of introverted personalities, poor interpersonal skills, and a feeling of inferiority when dealing with customers who (by and large) have more money and education than the bankers do. Finally, most bankers were loath to think of themselves as salespeople—a notion they perceived as better suited to employees on used-car lots than in bank branches.*

*Armed with these root-cause insights, training for bankers was expanded to include elements related to personality types, emotional intelligence, and vocational identity (recasting "sales" as the more noble pursuit of "helping customers discover and fulfill their unarticulated needs"). This enhancement not only put the program back on track within six months but also ultimately delivered sustainable sales lifts in excess of original targets.*

Even with a tight timeline, the team at OM embodied these principles during their transition to Virtuous. While they did rely on a vendor for training, OM also contracted for additional training time and scheduled follow-up, in-person training to ensure their team was well-equipped. In addition, they encouraged their core team to experiment in the platform before going live. Through this process, they allowed for the natural struggle that comes with learning a new skill, but they provided ongoing training with an internal team to supplement learning along the way.

## Incentives

We've said it time and time again — change is hard. But it can be almost impossible without a strong *reason* to change. Any successful change requires a strong "why" along with proper incentives that compel team members to push past their comfort zone.

Consider how many people struggle with adopting a new exercise plan. We've likely all made a personal resolution to get more exercise or eat healthier — and though we started the plan with the best intentions, we failed to fully realize the benefits due to a lack of motivation to stay the course. As the McKinsey & Company team pointed out, even the best strategies can't guarantee success when you ignore the psychological needs of your team.

When providing an incentive for change, it's critical to remember that you need incentives at multiple levels. It's easy to say, "Switching to this new process will allow us to acknowledge gifts 25% faster." But while organizational outcomes are critical to justify a change, they often do little to provide the personal motivation required to inspire your team. In most cases, broad organizational benefits aren't enough to justify the pain — or the *perceived* pain — of change for the individual contributors on your team.

We've seen this firsthand when working with our clients at Virtuous. Years ago, before we started offering more formal guidance on change management, we were working with a new client on implementing Virtuous for their team. The organization had already gone through a lengthy sales process before deciding that Virtuous best fit their needs. After spending time migrating data from their legacy system, providing training for the team, and ultimately going "live," they hit an unexpected roadblock: the one employee who was primarily responsible for gift entry said that it took too long to enter data into Virtuous. She could do gift entry faster in their legacy system, so she told the team that she wouldn't be using Virtuous.

It makes sense that data entry would be faster in a system a team member has been using for years. Data entry is largely about muscle memory, routine, and rhythm. And this user simply hadn't spent time developing that same muscle memory in the new system. But after a considerable investment of time and resources, one team member was derailing a critical change for the entire organization, and why? *Because they had no incentive to change.* This employee might have heard all about the fundraising or efficiency benefits of working in Virtuous, but as they saw it, this change would make their job harder in the short term, and there was no reason to change. For them, what they were doing was working just fine. No reason to change what isn't broken.

In this situation, it would be easy to blame the one persnickety user. But, in a very real sense, it wasn't the user's fault. The nonprofit (and the team at Virtuous) never helped create the right incentives to motivate change. The reality is that resistance to change happens all the time, in response to big and small changes. To effectively overcome resistance, it's crucial to fully understand each person's motivation to change, and then create incentives that help facilitate personal wins for each person on the team.

To help illustrate the point, let's look again at the successful example of OM and how they navigated a complex system change quickly. As we've already mentioned, OM began their process with information sessions that communicated the Vision of working in Virtuous to their entire staff. As part of this process, staff members were encouraged to share their concerns. These more extensive information sessions were followed by smaller group sessions within each department where concerns could be shared by those most directly affected by specific process changes.

The opportunity to voice concerns is not trivial. It's an integral part of managing any complex change process, and the sooner it happens, the better. I often say that it's best to "accelerate the pain" when managing a transition, meaning that it's better to uncover roadblocks early so they can be addressed as part of the larger process instead of stumbling over these hurdles when sprinting toward a final deadline.

Allowing individual team members' voices to be heard helps management quickly understand where resistance will arise and where incentives need to be created. And it also provides an often overlooked incentive in the change process: agency. As opposed to having change forced on them, each team member has some voice in the process and feels a sense of ownership from the beginning.

These smaller group discussions were also ideal opportunities to lay out more direct incentives for each team. OM tailored the vision of change for each group and let them know what improvements they could expect to see on a day-to-day basis. They admitted that the change wouldn't be easy initially, but they helped each team member identify a clear win after the change was complete.

## *Resources*

We've already discussed how important it is for every team member to receive ongoing training to develop the skills they need to adapt to new tools, processes, and circumstances. But training alone is not enough. It's important for everyone on your team to have accessible resources in the form of a community and content to remove friction along the way.

Becoming a parent for the first time is one of the most significant life changes for many people. In those first sleep-deprived days, new parents need to have a network of friends and family who have had babies of their own who are willing to give advice or pitch in when things get overwhelming. As the saying goes, when it comes to parenting, it takes a village.

Managing change for your organization is no different. Adopting a new strategy, program, or technology requires helpful resources that your team can rely on when the path becomes less clear.

Sharing the vision for change in a single meeting isn't enough — all known details of the change need to be documented and shared widely. Provide access to all documentation for all team members and empower everyone to review them at any time. Transparency and access build trust and agency. Ensure that there is ample documentation to support all training initiatives, keeping in mind that the best learning happens slowly and that learners who are forced to find their own answers will often retain information much better than those who are freely given answers.

The key to good documentation, as with any written material, is ensuring the content is clear and concise. But a well-written how-to guide is only valuable to someone who can find it.

Creating easy-to-consume documentation means acknowledging that your team members have different learning styles and they don't have hours to spend reading irrelevant information. There's a temptation to simply document every detail of your change in a 50-page Word document. The reality is that nonprofits are littered with hundreds of unread Word documents that become far too cumbersome to be useful. Rather than simply using a document dumping ground for all the information about a project, we recommend the following alternatives:

- Use short videos to provide summaries and screen shares of the key elements of the change

- Divide your documentation by persona (Finance Team, Fundraising Team, etc) so that teams can quickly find the documentation most relevant to their needs.

- Use visual Kanban Boards or Gantt Charts to dynamically illustrate the key owners, dates, and steps involved in the change.

But even the most precise documentation is useless if no one can find it. Discoverability is a real challenge facing organizations everywhere, and a lack of discoverability can hinder even the best change efforts. To be successful, every team member must know how to find relevant information and be able to access the content easily. Pin relevant documents in public Slack channels, create folders on company-wide drives with clear titles, and email access to those documents on a regular basis, consistently reminding team members where information can be found.

One oft-overlooked resource in managing any significant change is people. Specifically, which team members are the go-to resources for information about the change? Who is leading the change effort, providing guidance, and answering questions to keep things moving forward? In other words, who is my knowledgeable Change Champion who ultimately owns the success of the change? Answering these questions will require identifying the right people on your team to own the change, granting them the authority to make decisions related to the changes, and ensuring that your team knows who to ask for help whenever needed.

Looking again at the example of OM and their transition to Virtuous, one of the keys to their success was having a team member dedicated to change management. While migrating to Virtuous was a group effort (like parenting, it takes a village) with several stakeholders contributing along the way, having one very clearly identified Change Champion to own the project was a crucial ingredient in OM's overall success. The champion at OM was not only granted the authority and responsibility to affect change, but they were also provided with enough time and space to effectively equip the team.

## Action Plan

If you're like me, at some point you've gone to a conference and heard someone share some fantastic tips that inspired you. Maybe it was a success story based on a new process you can't wait to implement.

But then, you get back to your office and realize that your inbox has piled up while you were at a conference for three days, and what's worse, you have no idea how to get started implementing that new process you were so jazzed about.

All that inspiration quickly fizzles. Innovation is stifled by the urgency of the mundane.

The most inspiring Vision in the world, the most compelling Incentives, and the best Skills and Resources can all lead to the same fizzle without a clear Action Plan. After all, as Antoine de Saint-Exupéry said, "a goal without a plan is just a wish."

The best Action Plans are specific — and they include clear deadlines and owners responsible for each task. As with the other Resources needed to navigate change successfully, the Action Plan must be widely shared and accessible to everyone, no matter their role. A well-crafted Action Plan can serve as both a Resource and an Incentive. It provides guidance to team members on what they should be doing now (and what's next) and allows everyone to see when progress is being made.

The team at OM crafted and followed an internal Action Plan that allowed them to navigate their move to Virtuous in their limited time and stay on schedule. Their plan included clear owners and deadlines for every critical task. As part of the process, OM talked with the team at Virtuous and other similar nonprofits to create a baseline plan based on best practices. They then modified the plan to fit the unique needs of their organization and team. After the plan was set, the key champions at OM managed the plan with short cycles of accountability and inspection. Their diligence in plan execution helped ensure a successful launch while mitigating the risks typically associated with software transition.

## CASE STUDY
## BRADY JOSEPHSON AND CHARITY:WATER

Brady Josephson is the VP of Marketing & Growth at charity: water, a global nonprofit bringing clean and safe water to people around the world. Founded in 2006, charity: water has funded over 138,000 water projects in 29 countries around the world. Josephson joined the organization in 2021, bringing with him over 15 years of nonprofit strategy and growth experience.

Innovation has been a core value for the organization since day one.

"We talk about it as part of onboarding," Josephson says. "It's part of our ethos, it's part of our DNA, it's in our values, it's part of our founder's DNA. And so we probably have more conversations around innovation than a lot of nonprofits do."

This culture of innovation has enabled charity: water to expand its operations and capabilities exponentially, but it's not without its obstacles. And as charity: water has grown, those obstacles have only become more apparent.

"We're always innovating," says Josephson. "And then you get bigger and bigger and bigger. It used to be a smaller team in a New York office, and you could just go around the table and come up with ideas. And now there's a hundred staff members in 20+ states and multiple timezones, and you just can't do it the same way."

As charity: water grew, it became clear that the organization couldn't sustain continuous big, disruptive innovations. The mobility required to make and sustain such changes wasn't possible within a larger organization, and the number of things that needed to be tested, improved, or tinkered with grew with every new project.

So, one of their solutions was to differentiate between capital I Innovation, which is large, disruptive innovation, and lowercase i innovation, which encompasses smaller, continual optimizations.

"For example, we've got thousands of sensors installed on water points around the world that tell us in real time how much water is flowing through those water points every day," Josephson says. "So what used to take weeks of manual labor to assess, like well performance or a water point breakdown, we can now know in minutes. We can even automate a text message to go out to a mechanic who can be in the community to fix something in days that used to take weeks, months, or even years to fix. For us, that's capital I Innovation. It's disruptive. It's a leap forward for our programmatic work."

"But lowercase i innovation is about sustaining innovation on a daily basis. How do you improve upon your work? And the distinction is really helpful because so many times you go to a conference, or read a book, or hear a podcast, about innovation, and you're tempted to lump it all together. And maybe you do need some huge capital I Innovation, but there are tons of opportunities around lowercase i innovation. How you process data, how your teams function, how you position yourself in the market — all the day-to-day stuff where you're constantly asking, 'How does this get better?'"

Differentiating between disruptive Innovation and smaller optimization innovation has allowed charity: water to create more sustainable changes. The processes for making big, disruptive, company-altering changes are not the same as the processes for innovating the way Finance manages donations. The organization can continue to make innovation happen on all levels, without getting bogged down in the details, or taking on too much at once.

"It starts with hearing a small group of people describe a problem, and then responding, 'What if we don't do it that way, and do it this way instead?'"

For Josephson, it all comes down to simplicity.

"Not doing too much research helped," he says. "We didn't look at what all the other nonprofits do. Instead, we decided to do it our way. People spend so much time trying to copy other organizations, and that makes it very difficult to innovate. And the irony is so many people copy charity: water and that's the least charity: water thing you could do is copy what we're doing. Instead, we try to discover what the next thing is. What our thing is."

Once an idea has been proposed, it becomes an ongoing conversation and project. Decisions are made around what kind of innovation it will fall into, who is responsible for it, what tests might need to be run, and what additional research needs to be completed.

"The first stage is talking about it and naming it. The sensor water point was a bit more strategic. We knew, programmatically, it was a problem. There were stats saying around 40% of wells in Africa are broken at any given time. When we verified that number, we discovered it was probably closer to 25%, but that's still a high number. So we got strategic, asking, 'What could we do to fix that, disrupt that, change that?'"

But, as many nonprofits discover, it's easy to get carried away and excited by large-scale, capital I Innovation. You have to balance keeping the boat afloat and testing and running experiments to make change happen.

"We're still trying to find the balance between the lightning-strike vision and a little bit of research and systematization," Josephson says. "You have to do a little of each, but if you do too much lightning strike, you're misguided, especially at scale. And, to a point, if you spend too much time thinking and researching, it's too easy to end up with something that's really not that disruptive or even innovative."

That same balance is applicable to lowercase i innovation as well. Smaller organizations are able to move quickly and get their whole team on board with smaller optimizations and tests. But for larger organizations, it can be much more difficult disseminating the right information across the organization, and ensuring innovation is adopted efficiently and regularly.

"I'm a big believer in the idea that speed wins," Josephson says. "The faster you want to move, especially with larger numbers, it'll break down so fast. When you have hundreds of donors, staff, offices, operation sites, etc., you need a clean, simple, and easy-to-understand business plan that fits on one page. That simplicity is really important because you don't have the luxury of five people sitting around a table unpacking the nuances. It puts a lot of pressure on your systems and internal language to communicate the essentials across your organizations. So a lot of it is alignment, documentation, simplicity — these are underlying foundational principles to the testing, optimization, move quickly, small i innovation."

Key to managing and disseminating that simplicity is creating transparency in the organization, as well as breaking down silos between teams. When teams are separated from each other, they may be making changes, creating disruptive innovation, or failing to move the needle at all, in complete vacuums. So while the Program team is charging full speed ahead, the Finance department may be using older technology, struggling to get their reports completed in a timely manner, let alone innovate.

"We continue to work really hard to have a shared, simple roadmap, shared, simple OKRs because previously each team had their own," Josephson explains. "Sometimes they overlapped, and sometimes they wouldn't, but it was a recipe for disaster."

Additionally, charity: water has taken steps to make their team more cross-functional by testing "squads" that include staff members from different departments working towards common goals.

"So, you might be an engineer, but you're assigned to the Growth team. Or you may be a designer on the brand team, but you're assigned to the Marcom team. Each squad has its own roadmap with more singular goals around donor acquisition or retention or awareness. And then you have all the skills that you need within your squad, and you're not begging and borrowing from other teams, or putting in tickets that sit around. It's a cross-functional squad approach. We've piloted it with my team and it's gone pretty well. There are some flaws, but it's better than the alternative where you're always going to other teams begging for them to help. If you value speed, you can't do it that way."

Once innovation is decided upon, it opens up a whole new arena of possibilities. Now, decisions around what changes to test, what experiments to run, and what kind of data to collect, start snowballing rapidly.

"Nonprofits are not known for quick decisions," Josephson admits. "But when it comes to innovation, you need to make some big decisions right away."

"I think the frustrating side in running experiments is that you can spend a lot of time running low-value, low-lever experiments that don't move the needle. So it comes down to figuring out what you should do, what you should actually test, and how you manage risk. Again, risk management is something else that nonprofits aren't super great at. But I'd say those who have a higher risk tolerance or a better understanding of risk can make decisions quicker, and have a way better chance of creating small i innovations, sustaining success, or creating optimization programs that actually work."

How does charity: water sustain this level of change and constant experimentation? Agile plays a huge role in this process.

"Our approach has been velocity. In my early days, when I was new and experimentation was less structured, our goal was to run something like 40 experiments. It didn't matter as much if they validated, won or lost, or if they were high quality, but we needed to start flexing our speed muscle and learn what was good or bad along the way. And so, we've been in this velocity phase, and it's been great, but it definitely has its limit. So this next phase we're moving into now is a move to more sophisticated, high-impact tests where that type of analysis is more important."

"Pilot is a magic word. We're just going to pilot. We're going to try it. We're committing to it. It's amazing how the narrative changes when you say that."

## SUMMARY

Change is one of the scariest words in the nonprofit world. But fear of change should not be the leash holding your organization back from sprinting forward. Like climbing Everest, change is manageable when you take it one step at a time, and cheer each other on along the way.

When you start with a shared Vision in the world, create compelling Incentives, apply your team's strongest Skills and Resources, and are guided by a thorough and transparent Action Plan, suddenly change becomes less of a scary monster in the closet and more of a unifying process around which your team can become more cohesive and focused.

# BUILDING A DURABLE TEAM CULTURE

*"Never doubt that a small group of thoughtful committed citizens can change the world: indeed, it's the only thing that ever has." – Margaret Mead*

In 2016, banking giant Wells Fargo fired 5,300 lower-level employees for wrongful sales practices. In an effort to increase revenue, Wells Fargo sales reps had reportedly opened as many as 2 million new accounts without customer consent. The scale of unethical practices was widespread and mindblowing. A toxic culture had taken root within the Well Fargo sales team, and customers were being openly exploited and deceived to increase sales.

In the wake of the scandal, Wells Fargo CEO John Stumpf testified before the House Financial Services Committee. When asked about the pervasive unethical behavior, Stumpf said, "Wrongful sales practice behavior goes against everything regarding our core principals, our ethics, and our culture."

Stumpf's remarks caused corporate culture gurus around the country to shudder. His claim that the behavior of Wells Fargo employees was antithetical to their "culture" was disingenuous at best. If 5,300 employees were pressured to open over 2 million accounts without customer permission, then unethical sales practices were clearly deeply embedded in Wells Fargo's identity.

Stumpf failed to appreciate that the Wells Fargo culture wasn't just a section in their employee manual or a pithy slogan posted on the wall at corporate headquarters. Wells Fargo's <u>culture was defined by what actually happened day to day</u> within the organization. Culture guru and Mckinsey alumni Jon Katzenbach defined organizational culture as "the self-sustaining pattern of behavior that determines how things are done." In other words, culture is "how things are done around here." Despite Wells Fargo's insistence to the contrary, their culture was made evident by the behavior of their team. And, like it or not, the toxic culture at Wells Fargo started with leadership and trickled down through the entire organization. The "unethical" sales reps at Wells Fargo simply embodied the culture that was explicitly or implicitly communicated throughout the Wells Fargo team.

## WHY DOES CULTURE MATTER?

Culture guru and award-winning author Patrick Lencioni once wrote, "Not finance. Not strategy. Not technology. It is teamwork that remains the ultimate competitive advantage, both because it is so powerful and so rare." Lencioni's words are particularly relevant in the world of nonprofits. In a sector where days are long and resources are limited, teamwork and culture become the biggest levers for resiliency within cause-driven organizations.

The work of a nonprofit professional is hard. Burnout is widespread, particularly for program staff and fundraisers. The hard truth is that when so much of our focus goes into the cause itself, very little time and energy are left to pour into the health and effectiveness of internal teams. As a result, culture work and team-building often fall by the wayside, becoming an afterthought to the "more important" cause-focused work. Organizations are left with rapidly deteriorating morale and high rates of staff burnout that, instead of being addressed, often get chalked up to being a part of "nonprofit life." Like at Wells Fargo, leadership insists that the organization's culture is excellent, but the experience of team members on a day-to-day basis reveals the fact that the culture is fundamentally broken.

In my experience, most nonprofit leaders would openly agree that culture plays a pivotal role in their resiliency and impact over time. But building a durable and resilient team culture takes hard work and intentional effort. If you want to develop long-term impact, a healthy team culture can't continuously take a backseat to the "cause." Great culture doesn't just build itself.

It's not uncommon for new employees to join a nonprofit with a true sense of passion and excitement for the impact of their work. But the "Pollyanna" feelings and dopamine high associated with joining a cause-based organization fade quickly as the actual grind of nonprofit work sets in. When the job gets hard and passion begins to fade, a strong team culture will be the competitive advantage that sustains your team and drives impact.

Culture is more than just a buzzword or general attitude. It encompasses shared beliefs, common practices, friendships, and core values that unlock team effectiveness and ultimate impact.

When your team feels a deep sense of belonging and purpose, they are more likely to invest their energy wholeheartedly into the vital work of your cause over the long haul. Instead of acting like "employees" of your organization, your team will be empowered to show up as energized, healthy "owners" of the vision, ready to create real impact and innovation.

With that in mind, how can nonprofit leaders move toward more resilient and effective team cultures? What tangible strategies can we use to turn our team into our "ultimate competitive advantage"?

## ALIGNING VALUES TO BEHAVIORS AND METRICS

One of the biggest pitfalls I've seen in nonprofit culture is the disconnect between the organization's stated values and the key metrics that drive the nonprofit's underlying financial and impact model. Most nonprofits spend time creating mission statements and cultural values to align the organization around a cause-based vision — but team members often have little clarity about how those values relate to their everyday work or measurable outcomes.

For example, a nonprofit might express the following cultural value: *"Collaboration: We value working with our team toward the greatest impact."*

Sounds great, right? But the question quickly becomes: What IS the "greatest impact"?

Does the team even know how we measure impact? Do they understand the mechanics of the organization well enough to know what activities will drive impact? Are they clear on how collaboration specifically feeds into that impact? Is the team focused on a shared metric that will tell them if they are accomplishing their goal? Are team members openly celebrated when they contribute to that measurable impact?

These questions should seem obvious, but they are often overlooked in conversations about culture. As nonprofits, we want our mission and values to feel aspirational but then fail to put any real meat on the bone. As a result, team members are left pursuing slightly different goals with vastly different approaches...all the while believing that they are a good "culture fit" for the organization.

The net result is similar to playing tug-of-war at a family picnic with family members who don't understand the rules of the game. Your immediate family is working as hard as possible to pull the other team across the line — only to look up and see your brother-in-law and cousin pulling in slightly different directions. Despite your best efforts, you are left with frustration, exhaustion, and an endless sense that no real progress is being made.

To fix this problem, we must first acknowledge that our mission and values are inextricably linked to our organization's goals, metrics, and key behaviors. John Doerr, one of the all-time great gurus of organizational effectiveness, once said, "Healthy culture and structured goal setting are interdependent." Driving toward a great culture requires ensuring that your team is all rowing in the same direction.

Fulfillment at work isn't just about feeling a sense of belonging; it's also about feeling a sense of accomplishment. It's about knowing that you're working with a team to make a real, measurable difference in the world around you. And, making a measurable difference means creating shared clarity around WHAT you're

measuring, WHY you're measuring it, and HOW you win together as a team.

I've seen several ways that nonprofits have successfully closed the gap between their values, metrics, and key behaviors. Rather than providing abstract examples, I thought it might be helpful to share how we've approached this problem at Virtuous. While Virtuous technically isn't a nonprofit, the core concepts still apply, and I've seen success with similar approaches at nonprofits where I've advised as a board member or consultant.

Here's how the formula for metrics-based values works:

1. ***Lead with Numeric Goals*** – Before jumping into more "touchy-feely" values, tell your team about the measurable problem you're trying to solve. For example, "We want to build 2,000 affordable houses for single moms in Phoenix in the next five years." At Virtuous, we explain our core metrics and numeric goals as part of new employee onboarding and provide a refresher session to the entire team at least once a year. Our headline vision is to create $10 billion in net new generosity in the world, and all Product, Sales, and Customer Success metrics roll up to that headline vision.

2. ***THEN Tie the Numeric Goals to Individual Roles*** – Provide detail on how the overarching numeric goals relate to each team member. For example, you might say, "As a fundraiser, you'll need to raise $3.5 million in year one to fund 500 new homes next year. Also, because this need is ongoing, we need to target 70% gross donor retention and at least 30% per year in new donor growth to achieve

our goal." You should then have similar metrics for every team or department, including Program, Operations, Communications, etc.

3. *NOW Explain Your Values Through the Lens of Your Metrics* – Here's where those aspirational values come into play. Instead of sharing your value of "Collaboration" in a vacuum, you can now say something like, "Collaboration: We value working with our team toward the goal of funding and building 2,000 new homes. To hit our audacious goal, we will require Marketing, Fundraising, Program, and Operations to march in lockstep toward our quarterly and annual objectives. If we focus on swarming our teams around the biggest problems that keep us from reaching our goals, and collaboratively coming to the best solutions, I believe we can do this!"

4. *THEN Attach Expected Behaviors to Each Value* – Values on their own can sometimes feel vague and disconnected from everyday work. Attach sample expected behaviors to each value to create more clarity for the team on "how things work around here." Writing down expected team behaviors removes ambiguity and creates a standard framework for celebrating people on your team when you see your values in action.[4] For example, if we say that we value "Collaboration," then the related expected behaviors might include:

---

4   Thanks to the team at Gallaher Consulting for helping implement this approach at Virtuous!

- I seek to listen first, and I assume that I always have something to learn.

- I value the time of my team members and I show up on time and prepared.

- I take responsibility for both my individual goals and our shared team goals.

5. ***Celebration & Performance Management*** – Once values rooted in key metrics are established, leadership can manage to those values more effectively and recognize and celebrate wins as they happen. The expectations for how each team member's responsibilities roll up into larger values are clearly defined, making it easier to identify those employees who hit the mark, and those who aren't a "culture fit."

At surface level, leading with metrics before values might seem harsh or cold. But, in the world of nonprofits, the impact metrics are truly what matter. When your team feels aligned around shared, measurable goals, then your culture will naturally improve. I know this may sound controversial, but great nonprofit professionals want to win. They entered the profession to create real impact in the world. And great cultures focus on helping teams win together. Setting a clear roadmap of goals and behaviors for accomplishing the mission together is the first step to creating durable culture change.

## PERMISSION TO FAIL: KILLING FEAR AND JUDGMENT

As nonprofits begin to scale and gain stability, there's a natural tendency to avoid risk. Mature nonprofits are infamous for developing a general allergy to change once they've reached a certain level of scale. The reality is that most charities don't face the same competitive market pressures as their for-profit cousins and, as a result, the cultural muscle for innovation begins to atrophy.

To fight this type of institutional inertia, great nonprofits develop a culture of mutual respect that empowers team members to share their ideas without fear of judgment. Instead of punishing change-makers and innovators, nonprofits celebrate new ideas and and encourage continuous learning. They foster an environment where everyone feels valued and empowered to contribute their unique skills and expertise. This collaborative atmosphere not only boosts team morale but also ensures that the best ideas rise to the top.

In his groundbreaking work, *The Hard Thing About Hard Things*, Ben Horowitz writes, "Build a culture that rewards—not punishes—people for getting problems into the open where they can be solved." When nonprofit leaders either implicitly or explicitly discourage new ideas or punish failure, they are crushing a culture of innovation. Great leaders encourage and celebrate new ideas even when they fail. As strange as it might sound, celebrating failure creates an environment where your team feels safe to try new things, test old assumptions, and begin to truly innovate.

Becky Endicott and Jon McCoy founded We Are For Good in 2020 as a community for philanthropists, nonprofits, and fundraisers. Through their podcast and community-driven content, they have met, interviewed, and collaborated with hundreds of people in the nonprofit space, listening to their stories, learning from their mistakes and successes, and growing their understanding of successful philanthropy.

"I think one of the great drawbacks, at least in the 20 years of nonprofit work that I saw, is that the language and the frameworks are all baked in scarcity," says Endicott. "They're living in the margins and playing within a tiny little budget, and there is absolutely no leverage to dream, to try stuff, to take risks, to fail forward. And because the organizations have this mentality, there's not a lot of safety that would encourage people to bring thoughts and ideas forward because it's such a top-down, heavy sort of sector."

Creating a failure-celebrating, innovation-inducing culture requires a healthy dose of vulnerability — and, to be successful, the vulnerability has to be modeled first by leadership. If your leadership team is unwilling to try new things and admit failure, then you can't expect the rest of your team to take risks on meaningful innovation.

The discipline of vulnerability and admitting failure at an organization is caught and not taught. It has to be modeled. Daniel Coyle, author of *The Culture Code*, put it this way: "Vulnerability doesn't come after trust—it precedes it. Leaping into the unknown, when done alongside others, causes the solid ground of trust to materialize beneath our feet."

"There's a whole movement around trust-based philanthropy right now," says McCoy. "We also see the superpower of trust-based leadership. In teams where trust is present, it creates an ecosystem for innovation. That's where bold ideas take flight."

Endicott agrees. "Everyone who is soaring and doing well has one thing in common — they really do the abundance mindset work. They work on themselves, on how to be inclusive. They're great listeners. They work on confidence issues, on scarcity limitations, and they really own it. There's this lack of ego that comes from doing that work, and you're able to scale so much faster because you don't care who's getting the credit."

An easy way to begin shifting your culture in this direction is to simply change your language to create more safety around new ideas. Adopt words that provide your team with permission to test and explore. Instead of saying, "We are launching a new program," say, "We are testing a new idea." Instead of saying, "Here's how we solve this problem," say, "I have a hypothesis on how we can solve this problem." These subtle changes may seem insignificant, but they begin to let the team know that we all have permission to try new ideas and occasionally fail along the way.

Generally speaking, I love to use the word "hypothesis" when I work with nonprofits. I know it sounds a bit scientific, but it conveys something very important. Starting with a hypothesis communicates that, 1) you don't know all the answers, 2) you're curious, 3) you are hoping to learn, and 4) it's a test… so if you fail you still learn! The more you can embed permission to be curious and experiment with your culture, the faster your team will rise to the challenge and innovate.

## THE UPSIDE-DOWN PYRAMID: A BOTTOMS-UP APPROACH TO LEADERSHIP

Building a culture of courageous innovators who have permission to fail starts with building a bottoms-up culture of leadership. Ultimately, your organization will only be as successful as your frontline team members and individual contributors. And it's typically your frontline team who has the clearest vision for the actual problems that your organization is facing.

Your Program team is closest to the community that you're serving. They spend hours every day in the trenches working to solve real problems. Your Fundraisers have the best understanding of your donors. They have countless conversations with your supporters about their hopes, dreams, and passion for your cause. At the end of the day, your team members doing the actual work of the cause have the clearest vantage point for recommending changes. Your frontline team needs to feel empowered to affect real change. They need and deserve a seat at the table.

"It's the difference between management and leadership," says Endicott. "There's a shift happening, where people have been managed and told what to do for so long, but they don't want to run with a top-down heavy organization anymore. They want to be uplifted and empowered and have a voice."

The most helpful metaphor for this type of leadership is an inverted pyramid. The Executive Director is at the bottom and is accountable to the executive leadership team, relying on weekly input to make decisions. The executive team relies on their managers. And managers consistently take direction from frontline workers on what needs to be done. Ultimately, organizational change is driven from the bottom up.

This bottoms-up leadership style, or "leading from behind" as it is sometimes called, isn't a new concept. In fact, some of the top companies in the world are empowering their employees to drive impact at the ground level. One of the most well-known examples of this approach is Google's 20% Project. Rather than dictating every task for their engineering team, Google Founders Sergey Brin and Larry Page encouraged their team to "spend 20% of their time working on what they think will most benefit Google." For some organizations, this level of trust-based freedom might feel disorganized or even dangerous. But, by empowering innovation at the lowest levels of the company, Google has created an innovation juggernaut. In fact, it's said that two of Google's most successful products, Gmail and AdSense, resulted from the 20% rule.

The bottoms-up approach to leadership certainly isn't limited to tech companies. Many of the world's most impactful social movements took shape when individuals within a community were empowered to act. The great Nelson Mandela summed up this idea perfectly in his book *Long Walk to Freedom*: "A leader…is like a shepherd. He stays behind the flock, letting the most nimble go out ahead, whereupon the others follow, not realizing that all along they are being directed from behind."

I was reminded of this reality recently in a conversation with my nine-year-old daughter. We were talking about my job, and she said, "Dad, you're the boss, and you don't have to have any bosses above you." It was a flattering statement, but I quickly corrected her and said, "Actually, I have A LOT of bosses!" If I'm not consistently taking direction from my team, partners, and customers, then I'm destined to lose touch with the organization's needs, and my ability to make decisions suffers. My success as a leader is largely dependent on my ability to take direction from the individual contributors on my team.

Jeremy Vallerand, founder of Atlas Free, summed up this idea beautifully during our recent conversation.

"I believe that in life, it's as much about what you're doing as it is about who you're doing it with. That's one of the biggest misconceptions in the nonprofit world. People think it's all about the cause. The reality is, if it was just the cause, no one would stay in it if they were miserable. People are passionate about what they're doing, but also who they're doing it with. People come for the mission, but they need a team that believes in them, has invested in them, and has given them the tools to succeed."

"Nonprofits that make it all about the mission can become extremely manipulative and unhealthy fast, where people become a means to an end for the mission. But instead, we cultivate a sense of, 'Let's link arms with a group of people who are passionate about the cause and who believe in each other, and let's accomplish the mission in the best way.'"

## FLATTENING THE ORGANIZATION WITH AN ALIGNED TEAM

One fantastic tool to create a bottoms-up, collaborative culture is "skip level" meetings. These meetings allow anyone on the team to meet with leaders who sit above their direct manager (their boss's boss) — or "skip" down to meet with team members two levels below them. As a practice, I meet with team members several times each week who are two or three levels below me in the org chart. These meetings often create the most enlightening and helpful moments in my week.

Embracing this mindset and flattening your organization will mean fighting against "micro-management" at your nonprofit and providing your team with the tools and empowerment to solve their own problems. In his seminal work *Good to Great*, Jim Collins said, "The moment you feel the need to tightly manage someone, you've made a hiring mistake. The best people don't need to be managed. Guided, taught, led — yes." Great management and great culture require this open-handed mindset. The best leaders are always great coaches and fantastic listeners.

To effectively flatten your team, you'll need to hire amazingly talented people for each role. It goes without saying, but the more capable and culturally aligned the team, the easier it will be to distribute power throughout the organization. The single most important (and possibly most underrated) attribute of any nonprofit leader is their ability to attract and retain great talent. Great leaders are willing to hire and fire based on culture. They are relentless in inspiring smart, mission-aligned people to join their team, and then convincing them to stay even when times are tough. I think Daniel Coyle said it best in *The Culture Code*: "Hire people smarter than you. Fail early, fail often. Listen to everyone's ideas. Face toward the problems. B-level work is bad for your soul. It's more important to invest in good people than in good ideas."

According to Jacob Hancock, who runs a nonprofit innovation lab, your people are the key to your ability to fail forward. "It's all about the competence of your employees in the process of failure. Are you failing because your employees are incompetent? Or are you failing because your competent employees tried something unique? Two very different approaches. The second one you can learn from. The first one, that's a managerial problem."

You won't hear this from me very often, but when it comes to hiring, you should be selfish. Don't settle for mediocre or misaligned team members. Be patient and stretch for great talent.

"Play the long game," Becky Endicott says. "Innovators have a long-play outlook on life. They hire people intending them to stay on. The best nonprofits invest in good employees early, onboarding them in really interesting ways, and it has a crazy effect on their culture and community."

## REINFORCING YOUR VALUES INTO DAILY PRACTICES & EVALUATION

For your culture to truly take hold, it needs to be embedded in the everyday practices of your organization. I know this might sound like an old religious word, but I like to think of cultural practices as organizational "liturgies." Like liturgies in a church, your cultural practices are the understood organizational rhythms baked into your nonprofit's daily and weekly schedules.

These practices can be incorporated into how you run meetings, how you conduct one-on-ones, how you celebrate wins/failures, or how you allocate company time. For example, at Virtuous, we ask all of our team members to volunteer at a nonprofit for at least two hours every month. One of our values is "Display Radical Generosity" and our volunteer program becomes a monthly reminder that we take our values seriously.

One of the biggest missed opportunities to reinforce cultural values is in employee performance reviews. Let's be honest: nobody loves the performance review process, but it represents an invaluable chance to amplify your culture. In addition to evaluating employee performance based on results and activity, the best organizations evaluate performance based on alignment with values and value-related behaviors. During the performance review process, specific examples (good and bad) should be given about how each person has embodied the values of the organization during the review period. And as nonprofits, we should be courageous in hiring, firing, and promoting based on cultural alignment.

At larger organizations, you can also utilize Employee Sentiment Analysis software like Lattice or OfficeVibe to do weekly check-ins around team member sentiment, job satisfaction, and mental health. These tools can help quickly identify cultural problems within the organization, allowing you to address issues head-on before they grow.

At Virtuous, we also seek to practice Greenline Feedback, a term coined by Gallaher Consulting. Greenline Feedback simply means that we give every team member permission to provide candid feedback (with compassion!) to anyone else on the team. We encourage our team to speak up fearlessly and let other teammates know where we can improve. The feedback can never be mean or shaming, and it has to be given with the intent to help everyone grow. In fact, we often say, "It's not you against me. It's you and me against the problem." Moving in this direction will require creating a culture where everyone 1) is open to receiving feedback and growing and 2) doesn't fear reprisal for negative feedback. Whenever possible, we also try to tie Greenline Feedback to our values so that we have a common understanding of where the team is misaligned.

## THE IMPORTANCE OF CELEBRATION

The final piece of the puzzle in any great culture is celebration. A nonprofit's work is never done, and it's often hard to slow down enough to celebrate your wins. However, celebrating wins, rewarding team members, and recognizing excellence are at the heart of a great nonprofit team culture. Celebrations are an excellent opportunity to remind the team of why they joined in the first place. They provide a venue for looking back at the vital work you've accomplished and refilling everyone's tank for the journey ahead.

"It's valuing that everybody has had a hand to get the ball to the hundred-yard line. Every team player is important; they all have value, everyone has a voice, and we're taking care of people's mental health," Becky Endicott affirms.

Celebrating wins at your organization can take several forms, but at minimum, I'd recommend the following:

- A corporate gathering (at least annually) to look back on what you've accomplished and celebrate together. This should be a party replete with laughing, yelling, music, and tears!

- More frequent individual team/department celebrations (preferably offsite and quarterly) where team members can recognize great individual contributions on teams, cheer for one another and strengthen relational bonds.

- Consistent individual "win" celebrations using a shared communication channel. At Virtuous, we provide a "#wins" channel in Slack where anyone can recognize other team members for their efforts. Whenever possible, these wins are tagged to a cultural value or behavior to reinforce our cultural norms.

## CASE STUDY
### MEGHAN CRESSMAN AND NEW STORY

Meghan Cressman's story comes to us from our friends Becky and Jon at the We Are For Good podcast.[5]

Meghan Cressman is the new Director of Development at Merit America, but prior to her new role, she was the Senior Director of Development at New Story, an innovative nonprofit focused on solving the problems of global homelessness.

Cressman began her career in higher education, eventually moving from the university level to Teach for America (TFA), where she built and led the National and Annual Gift Team for K-12 education. If you're not familiar with TFA, their team deploys teachers to low-income or underserved school districts where educational improvements are needed most. During her tenure at TFA, Cressman became keenly aware of the fact that it was challenging for kids to learn when their most basic needs weren't being met.

When the school systems shut down during the COVID pandemic in 2020, she was struck by a horrifying statistic: 100,000 kids in TFA's New York City program vanished the day schools closed. Most of these kids were homeless, and there was no record of who they were living with or how they were going to access online education during the pandemic.

---

5   https://www.weareforgood.com/listen-to-the-podcast

This monumental problem led Cressman to New Story, a forward-thinking nonprofit pioneering solutions to end global homelessness. Founded in 2014, the organization has innovation built into its DNA. Their pioneering spirit is evident not only in the creative tech-oriented housing solutions (including investments in 3D-printing homes) but also in how the organization operates.

"At New Story, we dream really big," Cressman said in her interview. "There's a mantra that 'bold ideas attract bold people.' We are unafraid of boldness. You have to be when you're an organization working to end global homelessness. That's a huge, complex, and expensive problem that won't be fixed overnight. So anchoring and being unafraid of the boldness of the problem we're trying to tackle has led us to seek out the root barriers. Not root causes, but we focus on the barriers, on what's standing in our way from solving homelessness."

"The first barrier we've honed in on is the fact that the problem is so large. There are 1.6 billion people currently living in inadequate shelter across the globe. That number is expected to double by the year 2030. You think about the scale of the problem and the cost of the problem, and you realize a home is not a cheap thing. A $50 donation doesn't give someone a home."

"New Story believes deeply that we need financially sustainable and scalable solutions. Everything has pointed us in that direction. How can we be more financially sustainable, as there isn't enough pure philanthropy in the world to solve this problem, and then what can we scale through for-profit, market-driven forces?"

"The second barrier that stands in our way is the lack of innovation in housing, particularly low-income housing. We are committed from the jump that those who need innovation the most should get it first, not last. We work to test and prove innovation in housing products and in the financial market, opening up opportunities for individuals living in inadequate housing to obtain a loan, build a home, and secure housing."

The New Story website includes an entire page dedicated to innovation. It's core to the organization's operations and culture. But how does their commitment to innovation translate into the people, values, and day-to-day habits of each team?

"Our team is really unsatisfied with the status quo," Cressman said. "A practice we embody across the board is ruthless prioritization. Fundraisers on my team cut anything that doesn't raise money for New Story. I try to ensure that my team and I have the space to prioritize."

But prioritization wasn't just a buzzword at New Story — it was a daily habit that Cressman implemented in her calendar and modeled to her team. Her relentless prioritization of time and resources, along with her bias toward action, bled into all areas of the organization, aligning every member of the team to the real priorities of the cause.

"We, the leaders, have to model that behavior. We live it and then we look for it. And one of the big things we look for is a bias towards action. We have a core value called 'Team of Founders.' We believe everyone working here should treat New Story as if they founded it. They should be focused on finding opportunities to scale, to do something better, to eliminate things that don't work, to let go of things that aren't serving us anymore. And, to take big risks. People with an appetite for risk-taking is huge, and we've learned to probe for those things as we hire."

During her time with New Story, Cressman ensured that the organization's leadership embodied these value-driven behaviors throughout the hiring process in order to better identify and onboard team members who fit New Story's action-oriented approach and innovation-first mindset.

"We make sure we're really good at finding good talent. The search for talent is an underrated place to spend your time. It's a skill that's underrated, and it's one that I make sure myself and my team are good at."

That emphasis on hiring risk-takers also applies to the relationships New Story creates with donors. Cressman's team took a unique approach to donor relationships, separating donors into two specific groups to align New Story's innovation with its fundraising strategy.

"We have built our donor experience around two types of donors: donors who fund our operations and innovation, and donors who fund homes."

Most New Story donors are committed to funding operations, but a loyal group of donors was acquired with the express intent of supporting innovation at New Story.

"We have a small group of donors called the Builders who fund our operating and innovation budgets," Cressman explained. "We look for donors who have the wealth to donate and the generosity but who also share our tolerance for risk-taking and innovating. These donors come into the relationship with an understanding that New

Story exists to take risks. We exist to pioneer solutions to fix global homelessness. We are not going to hit it 100% every time. We're going to fail a lot, and when we win, we're going to win big. So we look for donors who share that mindset."

The Builders have proven instrumental in supporting New Story's commitment to driving new ideas. They start their giving relationship with a clear understanding of the role their donations are playing and the risks they are funding. As part of this initiative, New Story tracks traditional metrics like donor retention, but they also track a unique KPI the team calls "Big Swings."

"My team takes at least one bold, totally wild swing per quarter," Cressman said. "These have to be high seven- or eight-figure asks. Occasionally, they land, usually they don't, but every time we take a big swing, we level up, and we think creatively. It keeps us bold and sharp, and it forces us to tell our story better, to dream about what we would do with $50 million."

In this way, innovation and risk-taking are built into the culture of every team at New Story, including Fundraising. A cultural bent toward innovation is embedded in the way the organization hires, optimizes schedules, creates goals, and raises funds. Each team has a culture mandate to try new things.

"We have a mantra, 'rapid progress even over perfection.' So many fundraisers want to get things perfect. I would rather move quickly and have something slightly imperfect than move slowly and miss a big opportunity."

"Don't let a good opportunity pass you by because you found a good reason to be slow. Just take action."

## SUMMARY

Prioritizing team culture demonstrates your commitment to the well-being and growth of your team, which in turn creates a cycle of loyalty and dedication. Focus on tying your culture to specific KPIs and outcomes with your organization. Then, relentlessly hire great talent and get out of their way. Remove the fear of judgment and empower your team to do their best work. As your team members experience personal and professional growth within your organization, their satisfaction will translate into more effective work and increased innovation. The net result will be lasting connections and reverberating impact that extend far beyond the confines of your nonprofit.

# THE POWER OF COMMUNITY AND STORYTELLING TO DRIVE CHANGE

*"Wealth isn't always measured in dollar signs. We each have time, talent, and creativity, all of which can be powerful forces for positive change. Share your blessings in whatever form they come and to whatever level you have been blessed." – Jon M. Huntsman*

Almost every nonprofit professional is stretched thin. They feel under-resourced and understaffed. And in some cases, they no longer believe that creating meaningful growth for their cause is possible. When I talk with nonprofit leaders, most of their problems fall into one of two categories: a lack of people or a lack of money. I can't tell you how often I've heard, "We'd love to do that, but we just don't have anyone to work on it," or "It's a great idea, but we just don't have the budget."

In many ways, I understand these barriers. Staff and budget limitations represent very real boundaries for nonprofits. The best nonprofits understand these constraints and are hyper-focused on the few core priorities that will likely produce the most significant impact. In fact, a nonprofit's success is often defined more by what it says "no" to than by what it says "yes" to.

But what if I told you that, in many cases, these perceived budget and staff limitations don't have to exist? After years of working with limited resources, many nonprofit leaders develop a scarcity mindset, and their vision becomes limited by the capabilities of their current staff or the size of their current budget. But it doesn't have to be this way.

## THE MISSING INGREDIENT

As I've studied the differences between mediocre nonprofits and nonprofits with outsized impact, the most significant distinction is often the organization's ability to activate an external community around their cause. The reality is that most nonprofits have access to a group of potential ambassadors or raving fans who care deeply about their cause — and they are ready to mobilize. It's likely that for every ten staff members at your nonprofit, there are 1,000 potential donors, volunteers, and advocates who care deeply about the problem you are trying to solve...and are willing to jump in and help.

If you surveyed 100 people about their most memorable experience with a charity, most of their responses would likely include an army of committed fanatics combined with a compelling story. In fact, many survey respondents would likely convey their admiration for the cause solely based on the incredible camaraderie and community that accompanied their experience. The most effective nonprofits create a sense of belonging for their constituents. They invite their audience to join a movement of likeminded trailblazers who care deeply about the cause. And these movements create exponential opportunities for innovation and scale.

In recent years, a handful of nonprofit campaigns have multiplied their impact by inspiring their audience to step into a story and community that is bigger than themselves. The most memorable of those campaigns included:

- The Movember Campaign (No Shave November): Raising awareness for men's health.

- The Ice Bucket Challenge for ALS Research: Even though this campaign was sometimes criticized for being passive "click-tivism," the Ice Bucket Challenge allowed The ALS Association to increase funding for ALS research by 187%!

- charity:water Yellow Jug and Give Your Birthday Campaigns: To date, 17,000 people have used their birthday to support charity:water and raised nearly $9+ million for clean water.

- Pink Ribbon Campaign to Raise Awareness for Breast Cancer: The Pink campaign has been so successful that my son now has a pink soccer jersey for his club soccer team!

- The Sick Kids Foundation VS campaign: This emotionally compelling campaign focused on Sick Kids donor groups mobilized individual communities to raise over $1 billion in four years.

- Annual Dressember Campaign: Since 2013, Dressember has mobilized a community of 280,000 people to raise awareness and over $18 million to protect and free people impacted by human trafficking.

One of my favorite nonprofit movements was the #KONY2012 Campaign, created by Invisible Children. This cultural sensation culminated with a short film that ultimately became the most-viewed YouTube video in the world at the time. Admittedly, this campaign had its fair share of uncertainty, leadership stumbles, and unproductive moments. That said, it's hard to deny the unbelievable cultural impact that Invisible Children was able to create. More than just putting global pressure on the Ugandan militant Joseph Kony, the movement proved that nonprofits could mobilize a community of thousands of young people around a common mission.

Rather than tell you the story myself, I've asked Bryan Funk to talk about the #KONY2012 experience from his point of view. Bryan started his nonprofit career at Invisible Children and was on the frontlines of the KONY movement from its humble beginnings.

## FROM BRYAN:

On March 5th, 2012, I took the stage at a small community college in New Jersey on behalf of Invisible Children to educate students about the longest-running conflict in central Africa at the hands of Joseph Kony and his Lord's Resistance Army, otherwise known as the LRA.

For the last year, my team had been speaking around North America alongside Ugandan advocates to raise awareness and funds for the cause. And in the past two weeks, we had been pre-screening a film that went live on YouTube earlier that day.

A film called *#KONY2012*.

But this day was very different. The auditorium was packed to capacity as students filled the room to watch the documentary film that had ignited and dominated the conversation online. That day alone, over 1 million people watched the film, donated to our cause, and announced their support.

As I took the stage, I pulled out my phone and opened Twitter. "Well, everyone, the latest tweet I saw before I stepped on stage was from Oprah — and it reads, 'Thanks tweeps for sending me info about ending #LRAviolence. I am aware. Have supported with $'s and voice and will not stop. #KONY2012'. Can you believe that?!"

Over the next five days, 1 million views of the film grew to 100 million, and every local and major newspaper, news station, college, high school, and community around the world knew about Joseph Kony and his crimes.

This moment was not created by simply posting a video on YouTube. This moment was created over the course of ten years of dedicated, consistent awareness and community building by Invisible Children. They built a global coalition of what they called *"anonymous extraordinaries"* who believed in a world where children were not abducted in the middle of the night by Kony's LRA. And these supporters backed their beliefs with their time, their talent, their voice, and their hard-earned money.

So how did a small nonprofit operating between San Diego and Uganda garner enough awareness to spark the fastest-growing, most viral video in the history of the internet? In short, Invisible Children created a model that prioritized awareness, education, and community as the foundation of their economic engine.

## FROM AWARENESS FLOWS FUNDING

Invisible Children's core mission was to halt the atrocities committed by Joseph Kony, considered the world's most wanted man by the International Criminal Court. Their mission was rooted in the belief that if people around the world unified their efforts, even the gravest of challenges could be overcome.

In 2004, the founders of Invisible Children created their first documentary film and mobilized around this mission and belief. We asked our friends to travel the country in vans, screening the film and spreading awareness. But for us, the mission was deeper than just raising awareness — for each advocate, the mission was intensely personal.

And so one by one, Invisible Children began building their movement by touring high schools, colleges, places of worship, and community gatherings. We emphasized a message that every individual's voice mattered and that each of us had a part to play.

For 10 years, the movement grew from a handful of friends to millions of people around the world, raising millions of dollars.

## FROM AUTONOMY GROWS SUPPORT

Invisible Children's approach emphasized autonomy at its core. We empowered young people to be the voice of the movement. We even seamlessly integrated our narrative into the history curriculums in schools, further instilling a sense of agency in students. Through education, we created a groundswell of newly minted experts to become the movement's voice — and our strategy of fostering autonomy extended beyond the staff by transforming supporters into advocates.

This sense of autonomy had its most profound impact when it was given to the actual beneficiaries of our cause. We aimed to "give away power" and prioritize the voices of local heroes with lived experiences, knowing that the people on the ground better understood the real solutions. When #KONY2012 became a global sensation, its true essence was embodied in the Ugandan advocates who came forward to share their experiences.

For our strategy to work, we needed to adopt a holistic view of our audience. We not only raised awareness, but deeply valued the time and talent of every individual, emphasizing that each voice was invaluable in the mission.

## FROM VOLUNTEERS, LIFETIME DONORS ARE BORN

Invisible Children's primary message to its supporters was clear: Each person's time, talent, and voice hold immeasurable value. This ethos was exemplified by our "MOVE: DC" event, where 10,000 individuals converged at the Washington Monument, petitioning the U.S. government to take decisive action against Joseph Kony.

But our approach was also hyperpersonal. Each of the 10,000 attendees was paired with their respective congressional representatives, resulting in tangible face-to-face meetings. The group's united voice demanded action towards bringing Kony to justice and funding to aid programs rehabilitating child soldiers.

This approach culminated in the passage of two landmark pieces of legislation, allocating unprecedented funds to central Africa. And the results were entirely driven by the enthusiasm and determination of young advocates.

These volunteers not only backed the organization with their time, but they also opened their wallets. The average age of our donors was 16, with most donors contributing only $3 per week. Ultimately, educating and empowering our community fostered a sense of commitment that led to consistent and meaningful financial support. By centering their efforts on awareness, autonomy, and time, Invisible Children successfully harnessed the potential of young activists to catalyze genuine change.

## EVERY DOLLAR MATTERS

As part of their fundraising strategy, Invisible Children committed to translating every dollar donated into measurable impact. The organization used funds for programs like an early warning radio network system in Congo that alerted communities to rebel attacks. We dropped flyers guiding child soldiers on how to defect safely. We even used codes to tie donations to each flyer so that donors could witness the tangible impact of their donation.

Contrary to what many believe, #KONY2012 wasn't a slick marketing campaign. It was grounded in a deep, hyperpersonal conviction, and its success was the result of the grassroots efforts of thousands of committed people.

The goal of the #KONY2012 film was to raise awareness, not funds. The film garnered 100 million views in five days, prompted 3.5 million people to sign pledges to Congress, and, over the course of a year, helped raise almost $30 million in individual gifts, a 350% increase in revenue from the prior year.

The KONY movement sparked one-to-one personal connections. It valued time and passion as much as it valued money, and it celebrated milestones along the way with every donor. The net result of the bond between the organization and our community was critical in driving impactful change in the world.

*Bryan Funk*

---

For Invisible Children, building and unleashing a movement of faithful supporters was the key to unlocking outsized impact. If you want to create an authentic movement, your vision can't be limited to the capabilities and time of your existing staff. Breaking through the perceived barriers created by your team or budget will require mobilizing a faithful and focused community of talented volunteers, influencers, and doers committed to your cause.

In the words of Seth Godin, "Leadership is the art of giving people a platform for spreading ideas that work."

Creating this kind of community requires intentionality. It doesn't happen overnight or by accident. And it will require your team to think about your broader community as more than just potential donors.

## SO WHERE DO WE START?

We can learn several key lessons about "community building" from #KONY2021 and other similar viral campaigns. Fortunately, we don't have to extract these lessons ourselves. Leading sociologists have spent the last 100 years researching movements, and their findings align with what Bryan experienced during his time at Invisible Children.

According to Dr. Manuel Pastor, professor of Sociology and American Studies & Ethnicity at the University of Southern California, social movements require three key ingredients:

- A vision and frame
- An authentic base of key constituencies
- A commitment to the long-haul

To better understand Pastor's components for social movements, let's examine them through the lens of the Invisible Children story.

### A Vision and Frame

Creating a strong vision and frame simply means telling a grand story about the world and inviting your audience to see themselves in the story. Great movements include stories that point people toward a clear, common vision for a better future. They appeal to our hearts and shared values, allow us to put ourselves in the shoes of our "neighbor," and then drive us to tangible outcomes.

The #KONY2012 film did a masterful job of sweeping its viewers into a story. It starts with a dad trying to explain the atrocities of Joseph Kony to his young son. It then transitions to the stories of other young children in Uganda who were kidnapped by the LRA. To this day, I have a hard time watching the video without being drawn to tears!

Once #KONY2012 has your heart fully engaged, it transitions into a clear call to action. Rather than focus on the impact that Invisible Children is making, it tells the viewer that YOU can make a difference. It exposes the viewer to a broader community of people just like them who are standing together to bring down Joseph Kony.

As you begin to craft your vision and frame for your movement, it's critical to remember WHO your story is about. If you make your story about your organization, then it will discourage others from joining. Great movements include stories that empower the broader community to affect real change. Storytelling is about THEM, not YOU.

## An Authentic Base of Key Constituents

Building an authentic, viral movement requires pushing power down to each individual within your community. Your audience must feel a fundamental sense of shared ownership. This type of community can feel scary for many nonprofits. True movements take on a life of their own, and at some level, the nonprofit gives up control. All of the viral movements we described earlier in this practice — charity: water, Pink Ribbon campaigns, #KONY2012, etc. — created their own ethos independent of each organization. Their power came from the commitment and innovation of their communities. Releasing power and control is never easy, but it's worth it.

Creating authentic, viral communities also requires a means for frictionless peer-to-peer sharing. In my first book, I discussed the power of creating a strong "viral coefficient." A viral coefficient is a concept that consumer brands often use to describe the equation required for an idea to go "viral." To create this exponential growth, each new person who hears about an idea has to share it with more than one other person (on average). Similar to #KONY2012 or the Ice Bucket Challenge, once this coefficient exceeds one, growth is explosive.

For Invisible Children, the movement was almost entirely grassroots-based. The #KONY2012 video garnered an unprecedented amount of public attention, but the movement's beginnings were rooted in person-to-person connections in the years leading up to the launch. For me, one of the most powerful quotes from Bryan's story was, *"We asked our friends to travel the country in vans screening the film and spreading awareness. But this was deeper than awareness — for each advocate, the mission was intensely personal… For ten years, the movement grew from a handful of friends to millions of people around the world raising millions of dollars."*

The movement wasn't fueled by top-down, institutional communication — it was fueled by friends talking to friends.

As we've watched many of these viral campaigns emerge, we've found a few helpful tactics that can help accelerate the authenticity and viral nature of your movement. These tactics will be different for every organization, but they present a practical roadmap for building a community:

- Focus on creating memorable, shared community stories (member to member) that are heartfelt and allow your constituents to tell the story in the first person ("This is the impact that I'm making!").

- Identify a handful of key influencers (social influencers, policymakers, celebrities, etc.) who are already passionate about your cause. Provide them with easy ways to share your story that aren't primarily about giving money. Make their job easy and craft their message around the movement... not your organization. Like with Invisible Children, if you focus on building an authentic community, the donations will eventually come.

- Remove as much friction as possible. If your audience has to jump through hoops or fill out long forms to join the movement or share with friends, then your community will be limited to people who are already true believers. Make your next steps and calls to action as simple as possible.

- In the words of Paul Graham, "Do things that don't scale." I know this sounds counterintuitive, but the best movements start with authentic, face-to-face interactions. Start small and personal. Learn what resonates. Grow from there.

### A Commitment to the Long-Haul

One of the most interesting aspects of the #KONY2012 story isn't the video itself — it's the years of community building that happened before the video went viral. Most of the stories that we experience as an "overnight success" aren't actually "overnight" at all. When many of us learned about the civil rights movement in school, we assumed that the stories of Rosa Parks or Jackie Robinson were igniting moments that happened in a vacuum. The reality is that Rosa and Jackie were simply standing on the shoulders of the community of civil rights activists who came before them. Sparks ignite fires, but only when the hard work has been done to gather the wood and tinder.

For your nonprofit, your "movement" can't just be a quarterly campaign to increase gift response rates. You need consistent work over a long period of time. You'll need to bang the drum until you're sick of hearing it… and then bang it some more. Movement building requires your team to be patient and "long-term greedy." But it's worth it!

## BUILDING A MOVEMENT: LET'S GET PRACTICAL

Once you understand the fundamentals of "movement building," it's all about execution. Every movement or viral campaign is different, but there are several baseline practices that can add fuel to the fire. The following list outlines the disciplines you'll want to experiment with as you build your community. No two communities are the same, so a few of these tactics may not work for you. That said, they are likely worth evaluating as you lean into empowering a movement.

### 1) Create Compelling Content

Develop high-quality content that focuses on great storytelling. Lean into great imagery and short, heartfelt videos that can be shared easily. Use a variety of content formats, such as blog posts, videos, social media posts, and graphics, to engage your audience on different platforms. In each piece of content, emphasize the story and emotions you're trying to convey. Numbers are great, but the story they tell is even better. Where possible, brand your movement with simple words or one-liners that are used both to brand content and also create swag (stickers, t-shirts, etc.).

## 2) Leverage Social Media

This one shouldn't be a huge revelation. The trick is choosing the social media platforms — and sub-groups within those platforms — that your target audience frequents. Odds are, a community already exists that is related, either directly or indirectly, to your cause. Find out where they spend their time and what they talk about, and tailor your content to engage them. Expand your content to other mediums like podcasts or videos. Regularly post engaging content that draws new audiences into your movement. And don't stop with just posting! Make sure to comment, ask questions, and share content from others.

## 3) Build Community Engagement Using Field Marketing

Create in-person and virtual spaces for your community to gather, discuss, and share their thoughts. Host events, webinars, workshops, and meetups to foster connections among your supporters. Encourage members to share their stories, experiences, and ideas about your cause. Or, if you're feeling bold, load up a van like Invisible Children and take your story on the road!

## 4) Give Back to Your Community

Lean into offering real value to the people in your community. Provide valuable resources, information, and insights related to your cause. Offer exclusive content or perks to your community members, such as early access to content or special events. Make them feel invaluable to your cause, and personalize your givebacks as much as possible.

## 5) Acknowledge and Celebrate

Celebrate milestones, achievements, and anniversaries within your community. Recognize and publicly acknowledge the contributions and efforts of your most engaged supporters. Again, this isn't about celebrating YOUR wins but rather the collective wins of the entire community.

## 6) Collaborate and Partner

Collaborate with other organizations, influencers, or businesses that share similar values and audiences. Don't seek to control the movement. Be generous and share the stage for the greater good. Co-host events, campaigns, or projects that expand your reach and introduce your work to new audiences.

## 7) Be Authentic and Transparent

Be personal and approachable in your interactions and communications with your community. Your emails and social posts should sound like you're talking to a friend…not like you're doing PR for a corporate investor. Share behind-the-scenes glimpses of the frontlines of the cause. Be quick to admit failures and ask lots of questions.

## 8) Measure and Learn

Regularly analyze your engagement metrics. Track likes, shares, comments, and attendance at events. Use feedback from your community to refine your strategies and improve the community experience. You only have so much time in your day. Find out where there's a fire and pour gas on it. If something isn't working, then pivot.

---

## CASE STUDY
### AIDEN REILLY AND BEN COLLIER
### AND THE FARMLINK PROJECT

This case study comes to us again from our friends at the We Are For Good podcast.[6]

Aiden Reilly and Ben Collier are the co-founders of the Farmlink Project, a nonprofit that works to connect surplus food from farms to food banks across the country. The organization was launched in 2020 during the pandemic while Ben was still in college. The movement immediately spread like wildfire, and they've continued to see exponential growth ever since.

In 2020, Reilly was working as a documentary filmmaker. As the pandemic took hold, he quickly realized that COVID was creating a growing humanitarian crisis closer to home, and he began volunteering at food banks. Through Reilly's volunteer work, the team discovered an article in the *New York Times* detailing how farms threw away billions of pounds of produce and food every year. At the same time, their local food bank reported running out of food. At that moment, a lightbulb went off. The pair of friends decided to charge headlong into the problem by bridging the gap

---

6   www.weareforgood.com/episode/300

between excess farm production and the overwhelming community of food-insecure people in the U.S.

Farmlink began as a simple concept — match the food scheduled to be destroyed with food banks that need it. But the co-founders ran into their first hurdle almost immediately. The barrier was not that they didn't have enough food — there were 20 billion pounds of food going to waste yearly in the U.S. alone. But they lacked the resources, people, and, most importantly, legitimacy to make their vision a reality.

The pair started by Googling a list of farmers and then calling them individually to ask if they had excess food to donate. During the first 200 calls, they received a lot of hesitation and plenty of flat-out "no's." It took hundreds of calls before they finally connected with a farmer who told them he had thousands of eggs that he was about to throw out. They jumped on the opportunity, rented a U-Haul, picked up the eggs, and drove them to a food bank.

While it was clear that renting a truck and driving the food themselves wasn't a sustainable model, that first delivery opened up a whole new world of opportunities. And with the pandemic highlighting the issue of food insecurity, they felt the pressure to scale up quickly.

"We couldn't wait around to get official 501(c)(3) status. We couldn't wait around to get some truck company to donate trucks. We had to just do it, and then show people that it worked," Reilly says. "The second that we got footage of us driving U-Hauls with a big Farmlink banner taped to the side of it and said, 'Look at this, we've delivered 15,000 eggs,' and then it was 50,000 pounds of food, then people started to trust us and embrace us. And that started this crazy boom of attention and help that we got from all over the U.S."

As a filmmaker, Reilly knew that Farmlink had a great story to tell — they just needed an audience. But they were able to take that one story and image of a couple of kids driving a U-Haul full of food and build momentum that snowballed into a movement.

"I definitely didn't know anything about agriculture or freight. It was the first time I drove a U-Haul. But what we DID know was how to call strangers and ask them questions. We were comfortable saying, 'Do you need help? What's your issue?' etc. We learned that lesson from doing reporter work. And then we also knew how to take that intelligence and put it into a story that other people would pick up and be interested in."

Soon after this first big win, Aiden and Ben reached out to the *New York Times* reporter who had written the story about food waste that had initially inspired them. The reporter just happened to be working on a follow-up piece, and he graciously included Farmlink in his next article, giving the project a much-needed boost of legitimacy. The piece was an instant success, which spiraled into features on CBS, NBC, and more.

As a result of this tremendous media coverage, the donations began pouring in. The increased resources and legitimacy only emboldened the team to dream bigger. Shortly after media coverage, the team was able to successfully broker partnerships with Uber Freight and Chipotle to help scale the solution. The new alliances helped raise additional funds, gave Farmlink even greater name recognition, and provided access to a broader audience.

Their partnership with Chipotle was particularly important. Farmlink was selected to be part of the restaurant chain's Round Up initiative. In November 2020, Chipotle customers were prompted to round up the cost of their meal, donating the extra few cents to Farmlink. The Chipotle campaign created an incredibly low barrier to entry for new donors and advocates. While pennies received from each customer wasn't financially significant, the Chipotle partnership allowed Farmlink to impact an audience of millions of new people.

Suddenly, Farmlink was converting a community of millions to their cause. Their compelling story and low barriers to entry were helping Americans re-imagine the issue of food waste and ask the question, "How can I help?"

"We live in an interesting world," Reilly says. "You're getting asked for and pulled in 57 different directions every day. People build up pretty good radars and self-defense mechanisms to bat off these kinds of solicitations. And people just want to engage with things that are genuine and that they actually will care about and connect with. So that's what we're trying to do. We want to make an ask and say, 'Hey, your dollar can feed 30 people.' That's amazing. But to bring those people in, we have to tell a story. We have to engage with something that they're familiar with. And we love doing that."

The community that Farmlink created around its story has been the cornerstone of its success. And, in the early days of COVID, all of their community building took place online.

"2020 was the peak of finding a community remotely," Collier adds. "We were a Zoom, Slack, and Google Drive workplace from the start. And despite that, it felt like you had friends in communities across the country that you've never met in person that you actually were friends with. At the end of every term, we try to do a ceremony of sorts where we just get on Zoom, and people share what is meaningful for them. And I specifically remember one fundraising fellow, Louise, had kept a journal every single day, and she just wrote one thing: one good experience with Farmlink. It could have just been a conversation with a donor or something internal that made her smile, and she read it. And it was so emotional. Everyone just started sharing how much Farmlink had been this community for them."

"I think that when we started Farmlink, we didn't ever expect that it would create a community on a computer screen. But, you actually had people who were like, 'This is everything. This is the whole reason I'm up and not just in bed still.' And I think that I'll remember that for the rest of my life."

For Farmlink, authentic community isn't just the secret to the organization's initial success; it's the key to the future of giving. Farmlink believes that they aren't just changing the lives of people facing food insecurity. They are building a new generation of volunteers, donors, and nonprofit organizers who will go on to champion other causes and change more lives.

"We look at what we're doing at Farmlink as an amazing thing," says Reilly. "But we all recognize inside that the biggest impact we're going to have lies in what the people who come through Farmlink are going to do after. We have hundreds of amazing, smart, passionate young people who, whether their experience in Farmlink is six months or two years, might change the way they think about working in the sustainability space and about feeding people and helping others. And the more that we make this thing both relatable and culturally relevant, the more people we bring in from other industries to join us, the truer that becomes."

## THE IMPORTANCE OF STORYTELLING IN COMMUNITY BUILDING AND INNOVATION

Dr. Manuel Pastor's framework for building movements started with casting a clear vision for the future. And vision-casting is impossible without a grand story.

Storytelling is how we all make sense of the human experience. It's the mechanism for connecting our heart and emotions to our intellect. Stories convey deep truths about the world around us and help build "sticky" memories that inform our lives. At their core, stories make us feel like we're part of something bigger. That our lives matter.

In his now-famous book *Find Your Why*, celebrated author Simon Sinek says it this way: "Storytelling is the way knowledge and understanding have been passed down for millennia, since long before the invention of written language. Storytelling is part of what it is to be human. And the best stories share our values and beliefs. Those stories are powerful. Those stories inspire. Those stories are both the source of our WHY and the fuel that keeps our WHY alive. That's the reason companies that understand the importance of living their WHY make it easy for their teams to fortify themselves with stories."

The most impactful nonprofits understand the power of stories to move their mission forward. They allow stories about their impact, their founding, and their particular worldview to animate their team and daily work. And they use stories about their impact to inspire innovation and bring their donors a step closer to their cause.

## THE GENEROSITY CRISIS: THE IMPORTANCE OF STORYTELLING IN FUNDRAISING

Unfortunately, a generosity crisis has been brewing over the past several decades. America is seeing a decline in low and mid-level donors. In 2018, only 49.6% of U.S. households donated charitably, a significant drop from 2000, when that number was 66.2%.[7] And this troubling trend doesn't seem to be slowing down. "Individual giving has been declining as a share of total giving for several years. It dropped to 70% of total giving in 2018, which was considered low, and has steadily decreased since then, falling further in 2022 to 64%," says Wendy McGrady, Secretary/Treasurer of Giving USA Foundation and Executive Vice President and COO of The Curtis Group.[8]

Today's donor lives in a fast-paced and hyper-personalized world. Everything they want, from their favorite TV show to personalized medical advice, is available at their fingertips at all hours of the day. They never have to look far for the information they want — in fact, they rarely have to "look" at all. Most of the content they want

---

7   Indiana University's Lilly Family School of Philanthropy, "THE GIVING ENVIRONMENT: Understanding Pre-Pandemic Trends in Charitable Giving," (Indiana University, July 2021), https://scholarworks.iupui.edu/ bitstream/handle/1805/26290/giving-environment210727.pdf.

8   Glenn Gamboa, "Charitable giving in 2022 drops for only the fourth time in 40 years: Giving USA report," AP News, June 20, 2023, https://apnews.com/article/charitable-giving-decline-givingusa-report-becaca47cae4bc4f55063cc9f1c5865a#.

is served up in a personalized email, text message, or notification before they've even asked for it.

The for-profit world is frantically driving a stream of personalized content to each of your donors, from the curated recommendations of Netflix and Spotify to the personalized ads on social media. Your favorite brands tell compelling stories in personalized packages custom-tailored to your desires.

Unfortunately, the nonprofit world has been slow to react, and it's becoming progressively more difficult to earn the attention of donors and volunteers. Fewer and fewer inspiring nonprofit stories are able to break through the noise and drive action for the cause.

One of the most significant storytelling gaps at most nonprofits is the lack of individualized impact transparency. Nonprofits need a better way to bring donors close to the cause by sharing stories about the impact created by each donor's gift. In one study, 75% of donors say their giving decisions utilized information about the nonprofit's impact.[9] Millennial donors, in particular, desire impact and success stories, with 60% polled citing an organization's ability to show its accomplishments greatly influencing their decision to donate.[10]

Impact reporting helps create loyal donors who feel like they are PART of your cause, not just donors TO your cause. It creates

---

9    Colette Stanzler, "Informed Giving: Information Donors Want and How Nonprofits Can Provide It," Root Cause, 2013, https://rootcause. org/publication/informed-giving-information-donors-want-and-how-nonprofits-can-provide-it/

10   The Case Foundation, Millennial Impact Report: 2014: How Millennials Connect, Give and Get Involved with the Issues That Matter to Them (2014), https://casefoundation.org/resource/millennial-impact-report/.

a tangible connection between the donor and the emotional and personal aspects of your work. And loyal, emotionally engaged donors and volunteers are essential for any meaningful movement.

In his influential work, *Managing Donor Defection*, Adrian Sargeant lays out the top reasons why donors opt out of giving. I would highly recommend digging into Sargeant's research, but I want to highlight a few critical points.

Most donors stop giving for obvious reasons ("I can't afford it," "I relocated to a different city," etc.). But, based on Sargaent's work, a shocking number of donors opt out due to very preventable reasons:

- A lack of acknowledgment (gratitude for the gift)
- The nonprofit didn't tell the donor how their money was used
- The donor believed the nonprofit no longer needed their support

In my previous book, *Responsive Fundraising*, I made the case for developing more personal relationships with donors at scale to grow giving. The fastest way to build trust and personal connection is to follow up with donors to say "thank you" and tell them how their gift was used.

These same principles apply to your "not-yet-donors." Tim Kachuriak from NextAfter, a nonprofit fundraising consultant, says every potential donor is asking the question: *"Why should I give to you, rather than some other organization, or not at all?"* In other words, in order to attract new donors, you must build trust by meaningfully connecting each person to the impact of your cause.

The problem is that donors are less trusting of institutions than ever before. According to Gallup, Americans' trust in institutions is at an all-time low. They report that only "27% of U.S. adults [express] 'a great deal' or 'quite a lot' of confidence in core institutions."[11] This means that most Americans have lost trust in institutions, including nonprofits. To rebuild trust, leading nonprofits are downplaying the importance of the institution itself, and creating a direct link between each donor and the specific work that their gift will accomplish in the world.

By building this link, nonprofits can create a more emotional and personal connection with each donor. And personal connection is at the heart of generosity. Una Osili from the Lilly Family School of Philanthropy said it best when she said, "Donors not only want to understand the impact of their gifts but value organizations that intentionally foster meaningful relationships with their donors."

## THE STRUCTURE OF A GREAT STORY

From the dawn of time, humans have used stories to relay history, entertain, or create cultural norms. They have also used storytelling to bring people together, ground them in a common history, or unite them around a common goal.

The most successful nonprofits combine specific impact metrics with stories to paint a rich picture of how each donor is changing the world. Humans are intrinsically personal and desire a personal connection to the causes they care about. We are also story-driven

---

11    Jeffery M. Jones, "Confidence in U.S. Institutions Down; Average at New Low," Gallup, July 5, 2022, https://news.gallup.com/poll/394283/confidence-institutions-down-average-new-low.aspx.

creatures. Stories connect with emotional parts of our brain and help us make sense of the world more holistically.

In nonprofit fundraising, there's an old adage that nobody donates to save a million kids, but they will undoubtedly donate to save one. Specific and individualized stories help donors and volunteers understand the real emotional and personal impact of your cause. Your impact metrics can show off the breadth of your work, but stories help attach names and faces to your cause.

## CRAFTING A GOOD STORY

The structure of most great stories follows what writers call "The Hero's Journey." The Hero's Journey centers around a hero who embarks on a transformative journey, encounters challenges/conflict, and ultimately emerges into a changed (and hopefully better!) state.

The easiest way to see this framework in action is to watch one of your favorite movies. I love movies like *The Shawshank Redemption*, *The Lord of the Rings*, and *The Matrix*, all of which include unlikely heroes who face unprecedented challenges and emerge victorious and transformed.

For nonprofits, it's essential to understand your role in the story. You are NOT the hero! The people impacted by your work are the hero. But the good news is that any great story also has a mentor/guide. Think Obi-Wan Kenobi from *Star Wars*, or Morpheous from *The Matrix*, or Miss Honey from *Matilda*. As the guide, you are uniquely qualified to help your hero reach their full potential. And, as a fundraiser, you can invite donors into the story as co-conspirators who play an active role in overcoming conflict and creating transformational outcomes.

This framework can help create structure and depth for your nonprofit work that can captivate your donors and resonate with their innate desire for meaning. Your stories should use real examples of struggle/conflict in the world. The conflict should be as specific and personal as possible. They should then paint a picture of transformation for the hero as they emerge into a new and better reality.

## STORYTELLING AND INNOVATION AT PATAGONIA

Great storytelling can have a profound impact on fundraising and volunteerism, but it can have an equally profound impact on your team culture and innovation. The reality is that work at a nonprofit is hard, and resources are spread thin. Stories can bridge the gap by creating a type of cultural knitting that binds your team together and inspires everyone in your community to dream big.

Nobody is better at using storytelling to drive a culture of innovation than the outdoor clothing brand Patagonia. What began as a simple company selling climbing gear has blossomed into one of the most innovative brands in the world. Through it all, Patagonia has adhered to a single core mission: "We're in business to save our home planet."

Rather than telling stories about their high-quality outdoor gear and apparel, Patagonia's stories have focused on their commitment to bettering the planet. And that commitment is evident in every business decision Patagonia makes. The company runs ads proclaiming, "Don't buy our products," encouraging users to instead buy secondhand products from their lines. They operate a highly successful "Worn Wear" section of their retailer dedicated to reselling donated products. And in 2022, founder Yvon Chouinard made the decision to give away his ownership in the company to a trust "dedicated to fighting the environmental crisis and defending nature."

Patagonia doesn't just preach environmental awareness; they live it. And Patagonia's entire sales strategy is built in support of its mission.

Nowhere is this storytelling more evident than in the employee handbook turned bestselling memoir, *Let My People Go Surfing*. One of the manual's key principles was allowing employees to work flexible jobs to live their lives, pursue their passions, "catch a wave" — and then return to the office to focus on the company's mission. From the beginning, Patagonia understood the importance of a company culture that ensured each employee lived in support of the mission and story at work and in their personal lives.

Patagonia doesn't rely solely on advertising and employee culture to tell its story. The Patagonia team has launched a media company that produces countless movies and stories that connect its outdoorsy customers to its mission of saving the planet. These curated stories focus on Patagonia's hero (their customers) and Patagonia's mission (saving the planet) while Patagonia's products fade quietly into the background. The Patagonia website even features "Stories" and "Activism" just as prominently as "Shop" on its main navigation menu.

This counter-cultural storytelling approach has not only created a loyal community of activists; it has also spawned a series of brilliant innovations. The Patagonia Product Innovation team works directly with the Patagonia community and vendors to identify opportunities to drive environmentally responsible manufacturing. As a result, the Patagonia brand produces gear and clothing made from recycled plastic bottles and used fishing nets. The Patagonia Innovation team then releases their innovations to the open-source community so other vendors can share in the environmental benefits. To close the loop, Patagonia leverages its media team to tell the stories of suppliers and community members who are stepping up to make a difference.[12]

Giving away intellectual property and encouraging customers not to buy products may seem counterintuitive. But, Patagonia believes that its story and mission transcend the status quo of a typical clothing brand. By focusing on telling audacious stories about their community, Patagonia has created an innovative force for sustainable environmental change.

## TYING IMPACT METRICS TO STORYTELLING

While stories are powerful in building a community, the most effective stories are paired with clear impact metrics that foster trust and accountability. Depending on your cause area, "impact" can often be hard to define. While some nonprofits have clear outcome

---

12    Really Good Innovations, "Patagonia: innovation culture and sustainability - a look at their circular business model," https://www.reallygoodinnovation.com/stories/patagonia-innovation-culture-and-sustainability-a-look-at-their-circular-business-model

metrics (e.g. "Number of Children Fed"), many others struggle to put hard numbers around the impact of their work.

Generally speaking, focusing on clear, transparent impact metrics can create amazing clarity for your team, volunteers, and donors. In our chapter on metrics and goal setting, we talked about the power of aligning your team around clear goals. Great impact reporting provides a north star for your team, your donors, and the communities that you serve.

For most nonprofits, "Impact Reporting" has become synonymous with an "Annual Report." Impact metrics remain out-of-sight and out-of-mind for most of the year until a ten-page glossy document is created to send to donors.

While Annual Reports can be useful, the real power of Impact Reporting lies in three key areas:

1. Providing transparent visibility to your team and community on the true impact you are creating on a monthly or even weekly basis.

2. Identifying problems or opportunities that need focus to accelerate your impact. This means constantly asking the question: Based on the numbers, what activities should we stop doing, start doing, or improve to increase impact?

3. Quickly closing the loop with donors on what their work is accomplishing.

The more you can connect each donor or volunteer to their specific impact, the better. If a donor gives to fund a new school, show them pictures of the school. If they give to save a dog, show them a video of the dog in a new home. Make it personal. Remove the obscure institutional language in your communication and create a direct connection to the work that your donors have made possible.

At this point, you might be thinking, "I'd love to do this, but personalized, story-based reporting is a logistics nightmare!" I get it! It's not easy. But it's worth it. Building a loyal, authentic community is a shortcut to scale and innovation. Don't feel like you have to deliver real time, story-based updates to your donors overnight. In the words of Anna from the Disney film *Frozen*, you simply need to "do the next right thing." Focus on fixing issues at your organization that stand in the way of great impact reporting. You won't regret it. And, when done well, donor retention will increase, donor acquisition will increase, your teams will be more aligned, and your Program team will begin to feel the weight of their impact.

## CASE STUDY
### JOSH GUNKEL AND WATER.ORG

In Practice 4: Human-Centered Design, we discussed how Josh Gunkel and the team at Water.org leveraged their community to drive innovation through the WaterEquity project and Float app. The Float app was designed to democratize the funding of systemic solutions by allowing donors to easily contribute to large-scale clean water funds in a simple, easy-to-access banking app.

One of the biggest challenges for the Float project was finding ways to close the loop with donors and communicate impact. The Float app represented an entirely new way to engage with donors, and the Water.org team was forced to rethink how they communicated impact to donors.

Historically, Water.org had relied on generalized stories in their communications that might apply to any donation. However, the contributions made through the Float app were much smaller and were earmarked for specific projects, making it difficult to quickly track and communicate impact. Closing the loop with donors would require innovative new ways to gather impact stories and metrics that resonated within the app experience.

"Before Float, our stories and metrics were about the families that changed their lives by getting a water or sanitation loan," Gunkel says. "These were very impactful stories, but they were full stories that took years to come to life. They couldn't just be plugged into the app."

Water.org's objective was to encourage users to engage with the app frequently. But, the nature of the small transactions made sharing full-length stories nearly impossible. In addition, it often took years for Water.org to see the full realization of the impact from Float donations. If the team waited until the project was complete before sharing full impact stories, their donor engagement in the app would inevitably decline.

To solve the problem, Water.org decided to use a more innovative approach that required incremental storytelling.

"We had to break the impact into smaller amounts that could scale. Essentially, we tracked impact using an algorithm over time so that we could report on the incremental impact of any amount of money for any amount of time. Donors who contributed at least $300 with a 3-year commitment would receive a traditional impact story related to one family. But what about the user that contributed $50 for six months? What was their impact? What was the impact in the first week, and what was it in the fifth week?"

Making impact metrics feel relevant in this new context was a challenge, and the Water.org team had to get creative to truly understand their impact at a daily level.

"We looked at creating new metrics like saved steps to a water supply or toilet flushes. We also played with applying game mechanics to the experience and testing different messages to understand what resonated and what didn't. All while staying true to the actual measurable impact created by the donor's contribution to their impact account."

Water.org's creativity and innovation was driven by the needs of its burgeoning community. While many organizations would have simply relied on traditional, infrequent storytelling, Water.org leaned into new ideas to draw its constituents one step closer to the cause. They listened to the needs of their donors and collaborated with their community to reimagine how their amazing stories could be most effectively delivered.

## SUMMARY

There is an opportunity on hand for every nonprofit to tap into a broader community that helps to expand the base of support, drive innovation, and accelerate impact. The goal of building a community is to find the fans, advocates, donors, and volunteers who work shoulder-to-shoulder with your team. When we invite people into a movement, we empower an army of supporters who see themselves as key characters in our story.

Building an authentic and effective community starts with telling powerful stories that put the donor at the center of the solution. Scaling a movement will require letting go of control and focusing your energy on the true heroes of your story: your community that you serve.

PRACTICE 8

# GENEROSITY OPS: STRUCTURING YOUR TEAM FOR SHARED INSIGHTS

*"If the statistics are boring, you've got the wrong numbers."*
*— Edward Tufte, Professor Emeritus at Yale University.*

I recently worked with a nonprofit that had accumulated a massive list of contacts in their database. The new names were acquired through a high-value email newsletter, along with a host of other fantastic downloadable content. These contacts were fully opted into marketing communication and aligned with the organization's mission.

After learning more about the list of contacts, I started asking some seemingly obvious questions like:

- How many of these contacts also donated to the organization?

- What's the conversion rate of these contacts to donors?
- What content typically produces the best donors?
- Are any current or potential major donors reading this content?

The responses that I received were underwhelming — but not surprising. In a nutshell, the organization said, "I'm not sure I can answer any of these questions because our Marketing and Content Team isn't really focused on giving."

Unfortunately, this organization missed a massive opportunity to increase generosity because its teams weren't aligned around common goals. A "win" for the Content team was increasing audience size, while a "win" for the Fundraising team was increasing donations. As an objective third party, I could clearly see that these goals were interconnected and not mutually exclusive. The organization's engaged digital audience represented a massive opportunity for new generosity. And their content represented a fantastic opportunity to better encourage and inspire existing donors.

I've seen some version of this story play out at countless nonprofits. Well-meaning organizations miss out on significant opportunities because 1) their teams lack shared goals, 2) critical data is inaccessible, and 3) important insights go unshared. And at the end of the day, constituents are denied the opportunity to participate in the mission in a more substantial way.

If you've been around nonprofits for any length of time, you've inevitably heard a nonprofit leader say, "Donors are a relationship, not a transaction" — or possibly even, "Our donors are more than just checkbooks." Nonprofit leaders intuitively know that their constituents have far more to give than just money.

Your own personal experience giving to other nonprofits likely validates this truth. Our motivations, level of involvement, and advocacy around a cause stretch far beyond our checkbook. The community surrounding a nonprofit is made up of individual "whole" people with a unique blend of time, talent, assets, and social capital to bring to the table.

But, functionally, most donors DO end up feeling like a transaction. The communication they receive makes them feel like they are just another name in your database. They receive one-way email and mail blasts based on the timing of your nonprofit. And most of the messaging is largely disconnected from their specific interest or involvement with your organization.

I firmly believe that disconnected donor experiences resulting from misaligned teams and goals are one of the biggest inhibitors of generosity. And I'm convinced that there's a better way.

## SO, WHAT'S THIS HAVE TO DO WITH INNOVATION?

The reality is that game-changing innovation will accelerate when you increase giving and inspire a community of loyal volunteers. To be blunt, you'll need additional money and people to create audacious change in the world

Throughout our first seven practices for innovation, we've discussed the importance of aligned teams, clear goals, and data-driven decisions. These three principles are at the core of a healthy fundraising and volunteer program. Unfortunately, most nonprofit teams aren't structured in a way that allows these principles to happen naturally. Funding your innovation and scaling quickly will require rethinking how your teams work together — and even redesigning how your nonprofit is organized.

And so, our final practice is designed to provide a practical model for aligning teams to scale around these core principles.

## THE DATA AND DONOR INSIGHTS PROBLEM

One of the biggest barriers to shared donor insights and shared goals within a nonprofit is the lack of centralized data. More often than not, the Fundraising, Marketing, Volunteer, and Program teams use completely different software and tools to track their data — and nonprofit leaders struggle to fully understand how constituents are interacting with different parts of the organization.

We've worked with countless nonprofits where even the Executive Director and Chief Advancement Officer can't access the actionable data they need to do their job. And individual team members get stuck in spreadsheet purgatory, where data is constantly being imported, exported, and compiled manually to drive decisions.

One of the unintended consequences of process and data silos is the inability for nonprofit departments to see how their internal data impacts other teams. The Marketing team can't track which digital campaigns impacted major donor giving. The Volunteer team can't tell if they were effective in encouraging volunteers to donate. And the Program team has no idea which stories or program areas resonate with donors or how their work impacts fundraising. Inevitably, opportunities are missed and constituents drift away from the cause.

This frustrating reality is complicated by the fact that most nonprofit software is notoriously bad at integrating with other systems. Many traditional software platforms require a crowbar and chisel to extract relevant data. Given the complexity and hassle of integration, most data remains siloed, and critical donor insights remain hidden. Each team can only see its own slice of the donor pie (volunteerism, donations, digital engagement, etc.), and no one on the team has a complete 360-degree view of each constituent.

Without shared data, it's also nearly impossible to share goals and insights across teams. Each team is limited by their specific view of the data without context for how they might be contributing to larger organizational goals.

## INTRODUCING GENEROSITY OPERATIONS

Organizations in the for-profit world tackle these problems around alignment and data-sharing using a new type of team called "Data Ops" or "Revenue Ops." In companies like Virtuous, the Revenue Ops team sits outside of the other functions of the business and creates strategic alignment by providing shared data insights across the organization. They help coordinate and assemble data from various sources and then provide centralized, actionable reporting to all members of the organization. They also help identify small pockets of innovation or rapid growth within the organization and then help scale the innovation and learning across multiple teams.

For tech companies, Revenue Operations is a critical function for optimizing revenue generation. The Rev Ops team collaborates with other teams to maximize the effectiveness of revenue-generating activities. Their responsibilities include identifying and addressing bottlenecks, implementing technology, driving data analytics to improve decision-making, and aligning the sales and marketing teams to convert potential customers.

The importance of Revenue Operations within many scaling companies to drive bottom-line impact cannot be overstated. By streamlining revenue-generating activities and sharing innovative practices, Rev Ops can act as a core driver of financial success.

In many organizations, Rev Ops is also responsible for shepherding the "Customer Journey." They work across departments to connect the key touchpoints in the customer lifecycle while focusing on the most impactful outcomes. The Rev Ops team then helps each department understand how their actions help or hinder customers through their journey.

As a result, companies with a Rev Ops team are more tuned into customer needs — and ultimately in a better position to adapt to changing market conditions. And because these teams help accelerate the pace of innovation, they are particularly important during times of economic uncertainty or rapid change.

Now, if you've made it this far, you may be thinking, "Yeah, yeah, that's great for for-profits, but my nonprofit world is fundamentally different." Admittedly, not all for-profit practices translate well to the nonprofit sector. Nonprofits have different incentives and team structures that require different strategies than their for-profit cousins. That said, as we've worked with nonprofits over the past decade, we've developed a strong conviction that a version of this Rev Ops structure can work incredibly well within a nonprofit team.

If you work at a larger nonprofit, you might already be familiar with the concept of "Fundraising Operations." Traditionally, larger nonprofits have incorporated a Fundraising Operations arm to accelerate activities within the Fundraising team. In most organizations, however, Fundraising Ops isn't given the authority to work across teams or drive insights. Their role is far more tactical, primarily focused on providing operational support, prospect research, reports, and data updates limited to fundraising activities. As a result, their work rarely delivers value outside of the confines of the Fundraising team.

Rather than use the term "Revenue Ops" in the context of a nonprofit or relying on the traditional label of "Fundraising Ops," we prefer the term *Generosity Operations*. The word "Generosity" is more holistic, and it encompasses Fundraising, Marketing/ Communications, Volunteer, and even Program activities.

Like in the for-profit world, the Generosity Ops team sits outside of the other departments and becomes a broker of shared data insights and learnings across the organization. They allow nonprofits to connect the dots on how data is interrelated across teams and then surface opportunities to build more holistic relationships with constituents. They also steward and scale pockets of innovation by bringing the right leaders and team members to the table.

As a result, the output of the Generosity Ops team should include:

1. A clear, sober view of metrics that helps align all teams around common goals and outcomes

2. A set of shared insights that helps optimize the constituent journey and allows teams to better serve donors and volunteers

3. A strategy for scaling latent innovation and learnings across the organization

The result of these key outputs is improved team alignment, faster innovation, and increased generosity.

Nonprofit marketing guru Tobes Kelly makes the case for a more holistic approach to generosity in his outstanding blog, "Some Personal News." While he doesn't explicitly call for a Generosity Operations function, he makes a compelling case for a similar role that owns the entire donor experience to ensure that every touchpoint aligns donors to the mission of the organization. Tobes is one of my favorite nonprofit thought leaders and I think he does a fantastic job of explaining the importance of a more holistic approach to optimizing the donor journey. In introducing the concept, he says:

> *"The best customer experience in the world starts long before you ever make a transaction, and it should be no different for a donor making a single or regular donation. True donor experience includes the entire donor journey pre and post donation all the way down to the messaging and copy in your emails, creative in your online ads or offline activity, and products, plus things like any unboxing experience, the post donation email(s) and SMS experience, the cancellation of a monthly gift process, and yes, traditional donor support. Donor loyalty is all about how donors experience your brand, not just the extent to which they believe in your mission. Like "customer-centricity", donor-centricity is critical to any growth thesis."*

I couldn't agree more! Your supporters deserve and expect a unified experience from your nonprofit. In his article, Tobes goes on to make a case for a new "Chief Donor Experience Officer" role within nonprofit organizations. He recommends that this new role expand well beyond the typical marketing duties to include a much more holistic view of the donor journey.

I absolutely love this concept, and I'd love to see more nonprofits adopt this role within their organization as a first step toward a Generosity Ops team. That said, driving holistic innovation and improved constituent experiences will require more than just expanded marketing responsibilities (though that does help). It will ultimately require a cross-functional team that can assemble disparate data into a single unified set of insights — and push real innovation and change across the organization.

## WHAT DOES GENEROSITY OPS DO?

The responsibilities of a Generosity Ops team will vary from organization to organization, but it can be helpful to look at practical examples. In our experience, the work produced by a Generosity Ops team will often include:

- **Connecting Volunteer data to Donor data**. Information like volunteer name, frequency, location, etc. is connected to donor profiles, allowing your organization to better understand each person holistically and provide unique experiences for both donors and volunteers. This includes reporting and insights on how volunteerism drives giving and vice versa.

- **Surfacing Program stories and impact data to Fundraising/Marketing teams**. A consistent process for gathering and sharing program impact can help ensure that each individual is connected to the impact they are most interested in. Tagging stories (e.g. clean water, child impact, etc.) helps both the Fundraising team and Marketing team quickly source the right stories for each donor segment and better close the loop on impact.

- **Identifying Ambassadors/Activists.** Through social media, engagement, or event data, the Generosity Ops team can identify volunteers or donors with social influence, and then match them with opportunities that fit their superpowers. Having the Generosity Ops team surface data around social influence or other out-of-the-box talents helps each team communicate more intentionally.

- **Reporting on how Marketing, Volunteer, and Fundraising activities are interrelated.** For example, your Generosity Ops team might ask questions like, "Do personalized marketing emails drive more major donors to our website or just traditional donors?" or "Does a personal connection to someone on our Program team increase donor lifetime value?" Questions like these can be difficult to answer in silos — but they have the power to help shift priorities and drive tremendous value to the organization over time.

- **Create alignment by providing KPI visibility.** In many organizations, there is a lack of visibility to team goals and metrics. By receiving real time visibility into KPIs across the organization, each team better understands how their work impacts the broader mission.

- **Identify innovation opportunities within the organization.** Generosity Ops works cross-functionally to test and validate ideas using data. This process can include testing new fundraising strategies (e.g. peer-to-peer events, influencer programs, new media channels, social ad testing), new internal processes (e.g. data entry automation, donor services efficiency, volunteer recruitment), or new technologies (e.g. data/software integration, data warehousing/business intelligence, AI-based efficiencies).

- **Create enablement and training materials for team members.** Enablement activities help staff members quickly understand how all of the pieces of the organization fit together — and how their individual role impacts organization-wide results.

## WHERE TO START

The type of Generosity Ops team you should launch will depend heavily on the size of your organization. It's often difficult for smaller nonprofits to implement a full Generosity Ops team, but variations of this concept can work at organizations of any size. You'll need to experiment with what works in your specific context, but we've provided some guidance below on where and how to start.

### *Smaller Organizations*

Sometimes, even a single person or committee can have a dramatic short-term impact on streamlining constituent experience or identifying opportunities for innovation. Designating an internal owner of Generosity Ops as a part-time job can help create momentum and responsibility around this function.

Your new owner can start by creating a committee with key members from each functional team. For very small organizations, sometimes this will only include a Fundraising leader and a Program leader. For slightly larger teams, your committee will include major stakeholders from each arm of the organization. We advise, however, that your committee include no more than four to six members to start. The smaller size allows the team to stay agile and action-focused without being dominated by more extroverted members.

Rather than trying to fix every organizational problem all at once, this smaller committee should start by answering four questions:

1. Where is our data stored? Are there hidden spreadsheets with important insights buried in our organization's drive?

2. What core KPIs (Key Performance Indicators) are most important to the organization, and can everyone see them?

3. What data points are we missing? Am I able to pull together all the data that might impact our KPIs?

4. Can I get our data converted into clear reports that are easily accessible to the organization and tied back to our KPIs?

Once these questions are answered, the committee can then more easily identify the biggest opportunities for improvement. In other words, according to the data, what areas of focus will likely generate the biggest results?

The Generosity Ops committee then works in two-week "sprints" (see the Agile Practice) to find ways to better share insights, create KPI visibility, and bubble up opportunities to innovate or change.

All of the work done by the Generosity Ops committee should center around a measurable outcome. For example, the team might start with a hypothesis like, "By sharing Program needs in real time with donors, we believe we can increase the response rate by 15%." By creating explicit short-term goals tied to measurable outcomes, the committee can remain focused on delivering results rather than getting bogged down in analysis or activities that stray from the immediate outcome.

## Larger Organizations

For larger nonprofits, the Generosity Ops team can sit outside of your Fundraising or Marketing teams to maintain a holistic view of the organization. In many cases, Generosity Ops sits under the COO or a similar operational leader. There may be a temptation to organize Generosity Ops under your IT team, but we wouldn't recommend this approach in most cases. Many IT teams value stability and work within longer timelines. It's imperative that your Generosity Ops team maintains a culture of agility and remains focused on immediate outcomes and not status-quo processes.

In a perfect world, the Generosity Ops team would include a data scientist and a nonprofit strategist working together to connect systems and find ways to increase collaboration across teams. The data scientist focuses on centralizing data insights and providing business intelligence tools that each team can use to view reports and explore data. The nonprofit strategist works across departments to determine the biggest challenges and opportunities that might be solved by better visibility or shared insights.

Your strategist should have the mindset of a growth hacker. The term "growth hacker" was coined by Sean Ellis as a way to describe the person at an organization who is hell-bent on finding levers to scale. Earlier in his career, Ellis ran growth at Dropbox.com and now teaches about rapid organizational growth. Ellis wrote, "A growth hacker is a person whose true north is growth. Everything they do is scrutinized by its potential impact on scalable growth..."

Ellis' "growth hacker" is exactly the kind of person you want on your Generosity Ops team. Your growth hacker should be senior enough to truly understand your organizational systems, fundraising strategy, and budget constraints. At the same time, they should have an entrepreneurial spirit and be fearless in advocating for change.

### Accelerating with an Innovation Champion

One of the many benefits of Generosity Ops is that it can become a hub for innovation. This team's unique purview and growth-minded approach put it in a powerful position to find and scale innovation. In many cases, innovation only happens within small pockets of a nonprofit, and then the change stays confined to a single team. The new innovative ideas or learnings often aren't shared across the organization, and when they are, the new ideas can seem out of touch with the goals or experiences of the other teams. Without a way to connect the dots and push new ideas across the organization, innovation simply dies on the vine.

To help illustrate, here's a common example of how innovation can get stifled in an organization. Our friends at NextAfter, a fundraising research agency, often help digital marketers test and optimize fundraising email campaigns. It's not uncommon for a digital marketer to learn that their emails and donation pages with long-form copy perform far better than shorter emails or donation pages. This learning might feel counterintuitive, but the research often shows that reading more copy can increase the conviction of the potential donor and dramatically increase the average gift size.

I've seen multiple digital marketing teams come to this realization, and then begin to test longer copy to increase online giving results dramatically. Unfortunately, these insights and test-based optimizations are rarely shared with the direct mail team or event staff. While online giving begins to increase thanks to these more innovative tactics, direct mail and event messaging remain largely unchanged, and their results remain flat. Again, innovation never spreads and generosity suffers.

To help solve this problem, I believe that every organization should designate at least one "Innovation Champion" who is responsible for stewarding and scaling the best new ideas. If you have a Generosity Ops function, your Innovation Champion can help lead the team or, at the very least, work directly with the Generosity Ops team to launch new ideas.

To be clear, great innovation can come from anywhere within the organization. Your individual contributors will often have the biggest breakthrough ideas. Rather than coming up with new ideas, the Innovation Champion within your organization is responsible for identifying sparks of innovation at the ground level and then helping to launch the new innovation across the relevant teams.

Dave Raley is the Founder of Imago Consulting, an advisory firm that helps nonprofits grow and create sustainable innovation.

Before founding Imago, Dave spent 18 years at Masterworks, a full-service agency dedicated to helping faith-based organizations innovate, fundraise, and grow.

During his two decades in the nonprofit field, Raley has seen multiple organizations fail to break down silos and successfully implement innovative and responsive practices. Through his work, he's identified a few key mistakes nonprofits make in not successfully leading innovation.

"The first mistake I see nonprofits make is that there's no clear owner for the particular innovation in question," Raley says. "The way one of my clients put it, 'Who's sleeping on the cot?' Meaning, who's staying up and working on this? Who is personally accountable for it?"

For many of the organizations that Dave works with, each department adopts new ideas in a vacuum, which further cements the barriers between teams and the rest of the organization.

"But on the other side of the coin," Raley continues, "there's a lack of collaboration. When organizations do have someone in charge of innovation, they often encounter the lone-wolf syndrome. That innovator tends to view themselves as the only one at the table, the only person who's going to come in and make something happen. They aren't bringing together other people, other talents, to collaborate."

"Organizations need something in the middle. Someone who owns innovation AND can bring all the other people to the table."

We believe that the Generosity Ops team led by a true Innovation Champion is exactly the innovation "middle man" that Raley is describing.

## TROUBLESHOOTING GENEROSITY OPS

No matter which path your organization chooses, it can take time for a Generosity Ops team to become fully effective. For organizations that have long-standing team silos, launching your team will take patience. But to help accelerate the value of the Generosity Ops team, you'll want to work hard to avoid the following common pitfalls.

### *Analysis Paralysis*

There can be a tendency for Generosity Ops teams to get stuck in "analysis paralysis." Moving toward centralized reporting and shared insights can feel like boiling the ocean. Your Generosity Ops team must avoid getting sucked into large-scale projects that don't deliver immediate value.

For example, I've seen many nonprofits try to overhaul their entire software ecosystem before working to consolidate data or generate any usable insights. Rather than looking for short-term wins, they end up stuck in a two-year quagmire of technology change.

Admittedly, it's likely that your Generosity Ops team will be somewhat limited by your existing technology stack, and your team should continuously re-evaluate technologies over time. That said, rather than trying to re-architect everything all at once, the Generosity Ops team should focus 80% of their time on delivering immediate insights and fixing pressing problems. One great way to accomplish this goal is to work in Agile sprints with expectations around driving measurable outcomes every two weeks. This cadence creates an urgency for the team to deliver value — and ensures that the organization can pivot quickly to solve data challenges.

### Innovation Bureaucracy

In addition to analysis paralysis, Raley pointed out a second common mistake that has been an innovation killer during his career coaching large nonprofits.

"What often happens," Raley says, "when an organization decides to innovate, is they have too much structure on one side of the coin and too little discipline on the other side. There are organizations that get really fired up about innovation. They create a team, and a system, and get everyone excited to innovate. And inevitably, what happens is they end up with 'innovation bureaucracy.' They set up an awesome structure around innovation, and then kill it with overcomplicated processes and systems."

In the world Raley described, groundbreaking innovation quickly turns into, "Fill out this application, then go through this step, and this step, then talk to this person who has the real authority, and get it approved here." And in the end, teams spend more time jumping through hoops than achieving tangible results.

"But there's also the other side of the coin, which is too little discipline," Raley continues. "Those are the organizations that believe innovation is organic, ephemeral, you can't nail it down. They go with the flow, but there's no real plan. And true, many innovators are ideators and creatives. But they need to be paired with the discipline side; otherwise, there are a lot of ideas that don't go anywhere."

This balance of freedom from bureaucracy and intentional discipline is crucial for a Generosity Ops team. The hard work will be in creating actionable and achievable plans without stymying growth with tedious processes. By focusing on small, short-term wins, the team will begin to build organizational trust without having to overcome years of institutional inertia.

---

## CASE STUDY
## NATHAN CHAPPELL AND DONORSEARCH

Nathan Chappell is the Sr. VP of Data Analytics and AI at DonorSearch, a tech company that provides donor intelligence data and solutions to nonprofits to strengthen their financial capacity. He's also the co-author of the top-selling book *The Generosity Crisis*.

Nathan is also a prototypical growth hacker.

Nathan has been fundraising for 20 years, leading sophisticated fundraising teams and raising upwards of $175 million a year. But over the past two decades, he began to notice that his job was getting harder and harder every year. The need for new donor dollars was constantly exceeding his team's ability to fundraise.

"I think we got to a point where we realized we couldn't hire our way out of it," Chappell says. "We couldn't just hire more fundraisers and more analysts to solve the problem. We had to work smarter."

So, they worked smarter. Chappell's first move was to look at where his team could adopt more advanced technology. He dove deep into machine learning and began studying what the private sector was doing.

"I'd always look over my shoulder at what Google was doing or what Amazon was doing. I've always been an early adopter, but I knew those companies were leveraging the technology to provide efficiency and precision."

Then came the audacious challenge.

"Our CEO gave us the challenge of growing our fundraising by 25% without hiring new people. I don't think that's an unfamiliar scenario to a lot of nonprofit professionals. Many in the sector are working in organizations where the need for philanthropy continuously exceeds the ability to get it. And they're working with limited teams with little or no budget to fund innovative approaches to their work. So it made us rethink everything. We were rethinking all of our processes and figuring out ways we could leverage all of the data we had. For us, it was a massive learning curve."

As his team dove into the data, Chappell immediately understood his limitations. But within those constraints was a sense of energy and limitless potential.

"You'll never have all the data you want," he says plainly. "And it'll never be as clean as you want. But advanced technology now, even compared to five years ago, affords you a much better ability to use that data, because this technology is adaptive. You'll never be ready to start, but the formative difference with AI is that, by definition, the 'learning' aspect of the technology means that you'll also never be done. You won't build a model and then stop. When you adopt that mindset, it's very freeing."

Chappell's team began adopting different tools to access new data to drive fundraising decisions. One of Nathan's biggest wins was the adoption of AI. His team began leveraging predictive modeling to identify the best prospective donors along with the most appropriate timing and gift asks. He also began to investigate data-driven marketing automation as a means to help streamline fundraising activities without the need to hire additional staff.

In addition to taking advantage of newer technology, Nathan focused on utilizing his existing team more efficiently and appropriately applying each person's expertise and superpowers.

"For us, it came down to structuring the team to consist of Subject Matter Experts or SMEs. We had too many people pulling double-duty. Having SMEs be excellent within their respective roles vs. a free-for-all where everyone was doing everything, made a real difference."

Nonprofits are notorious for creating organizational structures that look like a Swiss Army knife, where everyone does a little bit of everything. But, spreading each team member across too many job responsibilities can be inefficient, particularly in larger organizations. When everyone is a generalist, it bogs down progress. The final work product is often mediocre, and team members don't have clarity around ownership (if the group owns it, no one owns it). As a result, accountability is lost, and the team never develops a deep expertise in any given function.

Chappell's solution within a Fundraising and Prospect Research team is a unique take on Generosity Ops. While his solution was confined to the Fundraising department, his suggestions were incredibly helpful in understanding the structure of a high-functioning team.

"I call it the three-legged stool, and I've built it several different times over my career. I look at prospect development as a whole, and within that, there are three different legs: prospect research, analytics (business intelligence), and prospect management whose role is to be the liaison of the data to the outside world. Every single request for either analytics data or prospect research goes through the prospect manager every time. No one's allowed to talk to a prospect researcher or data analyst because it will just waste their time and distract them from their main priority. This structure has created tremendous efficiency and also increases job satisfaction by keeping people aligned with the things they do best."

"What it does," Chappell says, "is it ensures that the data has a seat at the table. No matter the size of the nonprofit, the data needs to be at the table where leaders are making decisions. With the appropriate person present letting us know, 'Hey, historically this didn't work out for us,' or 'Our data says we should pivot this way,' it will make a huge difference."

"In fact," Chappell adds, "if I were a CDO anywhere right now, my right-hand person would be a data person. I wouldn't make a move without knowing what the data tells us historically and what it predicts for the future. I don't see organizations moving forward without having data-informed leadership."

In the world of modern fundraising, great organizations ensure that every team has access to all of the organization's actionable data.

"Historically, nonprofits have someone who's a gatekeeper of data and technology. That's not realistic. Every future fundraiser wants to be empowered to make decisions. They want confidence in the technology, and they want to be able to do it themselves. The future is all self-service. Everyone's empowered by data 24/7 — that's the world we live in. And technology is becoming better, more usable, and more user-friendly. That will translate into self-service insights, and will be the dealmaker for nonprofits that actually succeed."

## SUMMARY

The creation of a Generosity Ops team has the power to revolutionize how your organization increases collaboration, shares insights, and drives innovation. The outcomes produced by this team will very quickly increase data transparency, accelerate decision-making, and provide visibility into the journey of your constituents.

A Generosity Ops team will look different for every organization. The key to building a good Generosity Ops function is identifying team members who understand your data as well as your organization's strategy and goals. When possible, this team should be led by an Innovation Champion capable of pushing new ideas across the organization.

# PART 3

# THE RESPONSIVE
# CHALLENGE

# THE RESPONSIVE CHALLENGE

The world around us is changing at an accelerating rate. As nonprofit leaders, it can sometimes feel like the field we're playing on is shifting daily. Large-scale innovations in the for-profit sector are making it more challenging to connect with our communities and inspire action. At the same time, advancements in technology are creating exciting opportunities for nonprofits to solve age-old problems in new and creative ways.

The problems you are trying to solve are complex. Work in the nonprofit sector is impacted by socioeconomic conditions, generational shifts, cultural changes, and more. Progressing towards a better tomorrow requires new ways of funding your cause, influencing your community, and carrying out your important work. Thriving in this rapidly changing environment will require a new breed of responsive nonprofits committed to innovating and dismantling the status quo.

Effecting change and creating a culture of innovation can feel overwhelming. In talking with thousands of nonprofit teams over the last decade, I often hear staff say they desire this new reality, but getting started feels like "boiling the ocean."

The good news is that change is more achievable than you think. We see nonprofit teams taking action and making progress every single day. We've seen organizations take the first step to adopting responsive fundraising by transforming how they connect with donors. And we also see nonprofits scaling innovative solutions to solve some of the world's most pressing challenges.

Earlier in this book, I shared how our partners at Mel Trotter were able to dismantle silos and accelerate team transparency. However the impact of implementing *responsive* at Mel Trotter was far greater than just aligning their teams. Our team at Virtuous began working with Mel Trotter in 2020 to provide modern donor and volunteer technology that helped to bridge data silos, increase team collaboration, transform team culture, and open unparalleled access to actionable data insights.

To our delight, the team at Mel Trotter didn't limit their transformation to simply upgrading their technology. Their internal teams began to embrace a culture of innovation and reimagine how they might better solve the problems facing their community.

When our team was onsite with Mel Trotter, we witnessed all eight Responsive Practices in action. Here's what Bryan Funk from Virtuous had to share about his experience:

> *When we visited Mel Trotter, they were in the midst of a major reconstruction of their rescue mission and shelter following a successful capital campaign. We*

*walked in through the front door, put on hard hats and reflective vests, and began our tour of the new facility.*

*I slowly began to realize how profound the organizational and program changes were. The homeless shelter was being transformed into what felt like a hotel. We passed beneficiaries in the hallways who were greeted and welcomed as "guests." Their rooms were designed as upscale bunk rooms — outfitted to provide dignity as well as emergency security and shelter. Different wings in the "hotel" were designed to provide services at different stages of the journey from unhoused to housed, including healthcare and dental services.*

*We stood in a bunk room with the then-Chief Advancement Officer, Beth Fisher, as she shared, "What you are seeing is the downstream impact of changing technology." The room was so silent you could hear a pin drop. I was holding back tears.*

*The adoption of a more responsive methodology was impacting more than just fundraising. The transformation had grown to encompass operations, program strategy, and the organization's culture at large. And those changes were rippling out in visible and tangible ways to their constituents.*

*The last stop on the tour was Mel Trotter's workforce development program, designed to equip those experiencing homelessness with skills to secure future employment and transition out of the rescue mission and into Mel Trotter's temporary housing program.*

*We pulled our hard hats off and sat down around the board room table with the Fundraising and Marketing leads, Database Administration, Technology staff, and the CEO. What I didn't realize then was that I was about to see an early iteration of a Generosity Ops team. They walked us through their current operations and significant team changes.*

*Fundraisers on the team were given fundraising quotas. Much like a sales quota, quarterly metrics helped increase successful funding for the mission and provide clarity for the team. We also saw the team collaborating to ensure Mel Trotter constituents felt loved and known throughout their entire journey. Generosity in action!*

*Seth McLaughlin, Director of Development at Mel Trotter, walked us through how the team had automated donor outreach and back office tasks. My jaw dropped when he said, "We don't have a single automation workflow today that existed six months ago." This team was learning, iterating, and adapting how they connected with donors in real time! And they were using shared data and reporting across departments to make strategic decisions.*

*The Mel Trotter team was willing to lean into a more responsive approach in order to reimagine how they serve their community. What started as a willingness to create more personal connections with donors blossomed into a desire to drive innovation more holistically throughout the cause.*

*For the first time, I began to fully understand how responsive fundraising practices could help drive innovation and responsiveness across an entire organization. And I am now convinced that this approach represents the future of philanthropy.*

**Beth Fisher and Seth McLaughlin – May 2022**

Responsive nonprofits understand that outdated fundraising, marketing, and program strategies are contributing to the generosity crisis. Unresponsive fundraising tactics, manual processes, and internal data silos are preventing nonprofits from achieving their generosity goals.

At Virtuous, we are committed to growing generosity, and we believe that giving is fundamentally personal. Donors give when they feel a personal connection to your cause. Your donors are already getting thousands of hyper-personalized touchpoints from their favorite brands, social feeds, and news outlets — and traditional, generic appeals are no longer able to break through the noise. Breaking through the noise requires a more responsive approach to fundraising that allows your cause to build personal connections with donors at scale.

In the words of Una Osili of the Lilly Family School of Philanthropy, "Donors not only want to understand the impact of their gifts but value organizations that intentionally foster meaningful relationships with their donors."

We also believe that reimagining generosity will require more than just new fundraising tactics. Adapting to meet the needs of the modern world will require sustained innovation. The most successful nonprofits are breaking down team silos, driving toward shared goals, adjusting to the needs of their community, and building a culture of innovation. They have embodied the eight practices to drive innovation, and their impact is growing.

I'll say it again: Change is possible. More than ever, the world needs the work that you are doing. And creating the new reality that you want to see in the world simply requires the courage to fight the status quo, and the discipline to adopt the necessary practices for world-changing innovation!

# ABOUT THE AUTHOR

## GABE COOPER

Gabe Cooper is the Founder and CEO of Virtuous, a software platform helping nonprofits increase generosity. He is also the author of *Responsive Fundraising: The Donor-Centric Framework Helping Today's Leading Nonprofits Grow Giving*. Gabe has a true passion for creating market-defining software and helping charities reimagine generosity. After serving in a leadership role at a large nonprofit in the early 2000s, Gabe went on to help build a series of successful products in the nonprofit and for-profit sectors. His team's work has been featured by Apple, *The New York Times*, CNN, Mashable, Forbes, *USA Today*, and *Wired* magazine. Gabe, his wife Farrah, and their five kids live in Gilbert, Arizona.

# RESOURCES

SCAN ME

### Responsive Fundraising by Gabe Cooper

Responsive Fundraising outlines the simple solution for nonprofit fundraisers everywhere. Using real-world examples from leading nonprofits, Responsive Fundraising explains how to take the personalized, donor-centric, connection-building practices most fundraisers reserve for major donors and scale them to work for all donors using The Responsive Framework

Download a free digital copy of Responsive Fundraising: The Donor-Centric Framework Helping Today's Leading Nonprofits Grow Giving by Gabe Cooper.

Also available on Amazon and Barnes & Noble.

## The Responsive Maturity Model

Change is hard. And making systemic changes at your nonprofit that help build more personal relationships with donors at scale can feel like boiling the ocean. .

The Responsive Maturity Model is designed to guide you, step by step, through the stages required to un-silo your data, increase team effectiveness, create personalized connections with each donor, and grow giving at scale.

**Download for free at www.virtuous.org/model**

## Learn More About Virtuous

Virtuous is the only responsive fundraising platform designed to help you grow by building more personal relationships with your donors.

More than just a CRM, Virtuous fully integrates marketing, automation, events, online giving, portfolio management, volunteer management, and more to provide a single unified Responsive Fundraising Platform.

**Learn more at www.virtuous.org**